A BEGINNER'S BOOK
OF GYMNASTICS

SERIES IN HEALTH, PHYSICAL EDUCATION, PHYSICAL THERAPY, AND RECREATION

Charles A. Bucher, Editor

BARRY L. JOHNSON

Northeast Louisiana State College

A BEGINNER'S BOOK
OF GYMNASTICS

New York

APPLETON-CENTURY-CROFTS

Division of Meredith Publishing Company

6125-2

Library of Congress Card Number: 65-26735

PRINTED IN THE UNITED STATES OF AMERICA
E 48173

PREFACE

A revival of interest in gymnastic programs is apparent in many schools and colleges throughout the United States. This is partially due to the recognition of the fact that the majority of our physical education activity programs have been devoted primarily to running games and other activities which do not contribute enough toward upper body development. This emphasis on games which require very little upper body strength has pointed out a definite need for such activities as gymnastics, weight training, and isometric training. Proof of this need can be found in many of the recent studies which have been conducted concerning physical fitness. For example, the Marines Recruit Training Command which tests thousands of American boys who arrive for training, recently reported that 70% could not pass minimum standards of physical fitness. In the Kraus-Weber Test (a test of simple motor skills involving strength and flexibility) $57\frac{7}{10}\%$ of American children failed while only $8\frac{3}{10}\%$ of European children failed. Certainly the inclusion of gymnastics in our physical education programs will contribute greatly to the all-around development of our students.

While gymnastics is still struggling for a foothold in some areas of our country, it is interesting to note that in Germany and other European countries, gymnastics is widely participated in and is considered a major sport. For example, in a recent gymnastic festival held in Germany, there were approximately twenty-five thousand spectators and nearly three thousand competitors.

Because the competitive sport of gymnastics is unfamiliar to many students, resulting in a lack of appreciation for gymnastic exercise and interest in attending gymnastic programs, it was felt that a book for the student was needed as an aid to practical class activity. Thus, this book is unique in that it was written primarily for the student with emphasis on guiding students toward an appreciation of gymnastic exercise and a knowledge and interest in the competitive sport. Other key features include home exercises, interesting stunts (described and illustrated), emphasis on the safety aspect, and the presentation of some physical principles which represent the "why" of movement technique.

This book should not be misconstrued to be a complete book of beginners' gymnastics for there are many other stunts which could have been included. However, it is felt by the writer that there is a sufficient number of stunts presented for a one semester beginners' course meeting three times per week for eighteen weeks.

Keeping the above points in mind, it is the purpose of this book to:

1. Present a basic gymnastic program in those events which are most often contested in the competitive sport for boys and young men. While this book is geared to boys' gymnastics, stunts in chapters 6, 8, and 12 may be engaged in by both boys and girls.
2. Present material which might be employed by gymnastic teachers in making study assignments to beginning students in gymnastics.
3. Serve as a guide for a beginners' course of gymnastics on an 18 week semester basis.
4. Provide information which might be helpful to students in broadening their understanding and enjoyment of the competitive sport of gymnastics.

It is sincerely hoped that this book will be instrumental in helping more students to enjoy an activity which has afforded the author continued good health and many rewarding experiences.

ACKNOWLEDGMENTS

The writer wishes to acknowledge his indebtedness to the following people for encouraging and helping him to gain the practical experience needed to write this book.

Mr. Ed Anderson, Mr. Bud Sowell, Mr. Gene Towsend, Dr. John Piscopo, Mr. Gene Perkins, Dr. Guy Neson, Mr. John Nipper, Mr. Bill Pearson, Dr. Lloyd Russell, Dr. Ted Powers, Dr. Francis Drury, and Mr. Bill Bankhead.

I also wish to express my appreciation to the many fine teachers in the various gymnastic clinics who have influenced my thinking concerning the "how" and "why" of gymnastics.

Mr. Gene Wettstone, Mr. George Szupula, Mr. Charlie Pond, Dr. Newt Loken, Mr. George Nissen, Mr. Tom Maloney, Mr. Pat Yeager, Mr. Jerry Todd, Mr. Bill Meade, Mr. Frank Cumiskey, Mr. Sam Bailie, Mr. Vannie Edwards, and the members of the past three Olympic Gymnastic Teams who served as instructors at the Gymnastic Clinics held in Sarasota, Florida and Tucson, Arizona.

Special recognition should also be given to Dwight C. McLemore, Sonny Martinez, and Wynn Jefferson for assistance with illustrations and photographs.

Members of the Northeast Louisiana State College Gymnastic Team who were especially helpful in serving as guinea pigs for the stunts within are listed as follows:

Gene Huffty, Marvin Jordan, Jim Walker, Wynn Jefferson, Thomas Frazier, Sam Walker, Dwight McLemore, and David Adams.

This section would not be complete without a special note of thanks to Dr. George T. Walker, President of Northeast Louisiana State College; Dr. T. E. Holtzclaw, Dean of Education; and Mr. Alva Huffman, Chairman of Health and Physical Education for their loyal support of gymnastics at Northeast Louisiana State College.

CONTENTS

A Brief History
of Gymnastics

Some form of gymnastics was probably practiced even before our earliest records indicate. For example, it seems reasonable to assume that while early man may have had a purpose in crossing from one side of a river to the other by means of a vine or pole, he also enjoyed the sensation of swinging, and from this developed various acrobatic skills.

Ancient records and pictures in stone indicate that balancing and tumbling were practiced in some form by the peoples of China, Egypt, India, and Persia.

Records of early civilization in Greece show that gymnastics had a prominent place in the educational system of its men. However, it is only fair to mention that gymnastics in those early days referred to a wide and varied number of activities which we do not now consider to be gymnastics. For example, gymnastics referred to wrestling, boxing, track and field, and various other activities. Even so, records in literature reveal that Greek soldiers practiced hand balancing prior to going into battle. There are also many accounts of acrobats performing various stunts, not only in ancient Greece, but also throughout other periods of history. Although the Greeks gave us the term "gymnastics," it was many centuries later before it was used strictly to identify those activities which we now consider to be gymnastics.

Germany was a major force in the development of modern gymnastics. From this country came many leaders who contributed greatly to the present system of gymnastics.

The first teacher of organized school gymnastics was Johann Basedow (1723-1790). He believed that play and bodily exercise were important for normal growth and development of the child. A wide program of activities was offered, including gymnastic exercise and lessons in balancing.

Johann Pestolozzi (1746-1827) is considered to be the founder of free exercise. He developed a system of bodily exercises and arranged them according to difficulty and effect on the body.

The first book on gymnastics, *Gymnastics for Youth,* was published by Johann Friedrich Guts Muths. Guts Muths (1759-1839) served as physical education teacher for fifty years and is now considered to be the "grandfather" of gymnastics. Guts Muths taught many activities including such skills as rope climbing, balancing and a wide variety of stunts. While he believed that gymnastics had much to offer both boys and girls, he felt that girls should engage in a less strenuous form of gymnastics.

Gerhard Vieth (1763-1836) is credited with describing many of the vaults, mounts, and dismounts which are still practiced at the present time. Vieth was a strong believer in the values of gymnastics for students at schools and universities.

Friedrich Jahn (1778-1852) is recognized as the "Father of Gymnastics." The invention of the pommeled side horse, parallel bars, horizontal bar, and balance beam are a few of the many contributions which Jahn made to gymnastics. He is also credited with founding the Turnverein (German Gymnastic Societies) which spread all over Germany and eventually to many cities of the United States.

Adolph Spiess (1810-1858) encouraged both the inclusion of gymnastics in the school curriculum and the participation of girls in the activity. It was through his efforts that gymnastics became a school subject in Switzerland and in Germany. Spiess placed considerable stress on gymnastic exhibitions as a means of holding the interest of students and also of selling his program to the public. Unlike Jahn, he devoted special attention to free exercise as a valuable event for girls and young children.

Gymnastic leaders from countries other than Germany who contributed to the development of gymnastics are discussed below.

Francis Amoros (1770-1848) was a Spaniard who served as national director of gymnastics in France. He was probably the first to use the trapeze and rings as a form of gymnastics.

Franz Nachtegall (1777-1847) served as Director of Gymnastics for all Denmark. Nachtegall also directed the first recorded training school established for the purpose of training gymnastic teachers.

Per Henrik Ling (1776-1839), a major figure in the evolution of Swedish gymnastics, developed a therapeutic and corrective system of gymnastics. He believed that gymnastics should be based on a thorough knowledge of the effects of the various exercises on the human body; and that gymnastic instructors should know physiologically and structurally why they teach each exercise. Needless to say, this system was too formal and contributed very little to the competitive sport.

Archibald Maclaren (1820-1884) served as director of military gymnastics for Great Britain in the 1860's. He believed that the popular games of England could not produce a well-developed body without the inclusion of gymnastics. Practically all of Maclaren's followers were in the army and consequently made the program unpopular by formalizing it into more of a military drill.

The development of gymnastics in the United States received its principal impetus from the German turners who settled in this country. Dr. Charles Beck, a German immigrant, established the first program of German gymnastics in the United States in 1824. In 1826, Charles Follen, another German turner, set up a gymnastic program at Harvard University and established the first gymnasium in the United States.

Because of political pressures, thousands of German citizens migrated to the United States in the late 1840's. This led to the establishment of many Turnverein Societies throughout the North. These societies promoted physical education by sponsoring outdoor games, gymnastic meets, and exhibitions. The American Turners held the first national gymnastic meet in Philadelphia in 1851, with awards and honors bestowed on the victors.

In 1865, the Turners established The Normal College of the American Gymnastic Union at Indianapolis for the purpose of training teachers of gymnastics. In the years which followed, they took advantage of every opportunity to sell their program of gymnastics to the schools. And in many schools, gymnastics became the physical education program.

After World War I, the school physical education programs began to lean toward the lighter recreational types of activities. These popular team games soon crowded gymnastics out of the program and as a result the fitness and strength in the upper-body regions of the American male dropped to a new low, as may be observed in the records of Army induction centers of World War II.

During the years between World War I and World War II, gymnastics managed to stay alive primarily through the efforts of such groups as Turner Clubs, YMCA's, Sokol Clubs, Swiss Gymnastic Societies, and a few colleges and universities. During World War II, military leaders recognized the need for gymnastic activities in the physical training programs. This revival of gymnastics coupled with the development of a new piece of popular gymnastic equipment called the "Nissen Trampoline" (1939), resulted in many schools incorporating gymnastics into their physical education programs.

Only once in the long history of the Olympic Games has the United States led in team scoring in the gymnastic competition. In 1904, the United States team led by Anton Heida, captured every event in the gymnastic competition. Heida won the side horse, all-around, and tied for first place in the long horse and horizontal bar. Other winners were George Eyser who won parallel bars, rope climb, and tied for first with Heida on the long horse; Herman Glass won rings; and Ed Hennig won club swinging and tied for first place on horizontal bar with Heida.

Frank Kriz was the only gymnast from the United States to win an Olympic title between 1904 and 1932. Kriz placed first in the long-horse event in 1924.

In 1932 the United States fielded a strong Olympic gymnastic team which won most of the first places, but failed to score enough team points for the unofficial team title. Winners from the United States in the 1932 Olympics are listed as follows with the events which they won:

Dallas Bixler	Horizontal Bar
George Gulack	Rings
Raymond H. Bass	Rope Climb
George Roth	Club Swinging
Rowland Wolfe	Tumbling

At present, club swinging, rope climb, and tumbling have been dropped from Olympic gymnastic competition.

Since 1932, the United States has failed to produce an Olypmic champion in gymnastics. However, a much improved 1960 United States Olympic Team placed fifth out of thirty-three nations and outscored such prominent gymnastic countries as Finland, Germany, and Switzerland. In 1964, the United States Team dropped into seventh place and such criticism as lack of team effort and friction among A.A.U. officials were given as the cause.

The growth of gymnastics in the United States has been tremendous since

1950. Three organizations which have contributed greatly to this expansion, by disseminating new ideas and by bringing gymnasts from all sections of the country closer together, are The National Gymnastic Clinic, The Western Gymnastic Clinic, and *The Modern Gymnast*.

The National Gymnastic Clinic was founded by Lyle Wesler, Gymnastic coach of Georgia Tech, on December 18, 1950. This clinic which started with some 35 people now draws hundreds of gymnasts and fans from all over the United States and Canada to beautiful Sarasota, Florida each December.

The Western Gymnastic Clinic was organized under the direction of Mr. Sam Bailie, gymnastic coach of the University of Arizona, in December, 1961. This clinic is now recognized as the largest in the United States and is held each year in Tucson, Arizona.

The Modern Gymnast is a gymnastic magazine containing national and international gymnastic news, photos, competition results, and instructions for men, women, and children. Mr. Glenn Sundby, the editor and publisher, has truly made an outstanding contribution to the sport through his publication.

Other organizations and developments which have contributed to the interest of the sport during the 1950's are the National Association of Gymnastic Coaches, the inclusion of gymnastics in the Helms Hall of Fame, the establishment of an all-American gymnastic team, the foreign gymnastic teams' tours, and the many local gymnastic clinics held in all sections of the country.

At the beginning of the 1960's a fight for control of power in the sport of gymnastics, as well as in other sports, developed between the Amateur Athletic Union and many of the collegiate coaches in the United States. The differences which existed between the two groups led to the founding of the United States Gymnastic Federation. While this organization has brought about a number of new and valuable changes in the sport, it is hoped by many followers that differences can be settled between the two opposing groups in the best interests of gymnastics.

At the approach of the 1968 Olympics, gymnastics has continued to grow at a rapid pace and become more exciting with each passing year. Perhaps one of the greatest lessons we can learn from a history of gymnastics is that too much formality in our instructional programs can destroy the interest and fun which our students should derive from this activity.

2

Competition

Gymnastic competition has a tremendous amount of potential spectator appeal. Evidence of this can be seen in the large audiences that witness the dual and championship meets at Penn State University. Also, records indicate that thou-

sands regularly attend various meets and festivals held in Germany and other European countries.

Perhaps, the most significant reason why gymnastics is considered a minor sport rather than a major sport in the United States today, is because coaches and officials have failed to capitalize on this latent spectator appeal. For example, the author has competed in many championship meets which required five to six hours to run off. Spectators soon tire after two hours regardless of the sport;

therefore, dual meets and the finals of championship meets should be run off in 1½ to 2 hours. This necessitates the use of preliminaries to determine the top six performers in each event. The preliminaries should be closed to spectators, thus allowing the public to view only the finalists in a 1½ hour evening performance. In certain events, such as long-horse vaulting, and tumbling, it might be advisable to further speed up the meet by allowing only the top three performers of the preliminaries to compete for first, second, and third in the evening performance.

Another important point to consider is the separation of men's and women's

competition. Gymnastics is growing too big to have both men and the women compete at the same time and place. However, it would be beneficial to each group to have an outstanding performer or two from the opposite sex perform an exhibition between the competitive events. This would indeed contribute to spectator appeal.

GENERAL RULES OF COMPETITION

The following rules are presented for the purpose of acquainting beginning students in gymnastics with a general knowledge of competitive procedure. An official *Amateur Athletic Union* [1] or *National Collegiate Athletic Association* [2] *Rules Book* should be referred to for more detailed information concerning the conduct of official meets.

1. The following events are normally contested in most meets: free exercise, side horse, horizontal bar, parallel bars, still rings, long horse, all-around, tumbling, and rebound tumbling.
2. Individuals entered in the all-around event must compete in: free exercise, side horse, horizontal bar, parallel bars, still rings, and long horse. The total score of these six events determines the winner and the placing of the runner-ups in the all-around event.
3. The competitors in each event (except the all-around) will receive their competitive order by drawing. This drawing is performed by the host coach in the presence of another meet official.

4. In dual competition, each team is limited to three performers in each event. If planning to compete in the all-around event, each team may enter one all-around man and two specialists in each of the all-around events. Only three performers may enter the special events which include rebound tumbling and tumbling.

5. Five places are scored in dual meets and team points are awarded as follows: 6 points for first, 4 points for second, 3 points for third, 2 points for fourth, and 1 point for fifth place. In case of a tie for a place, the total points for the place tied for and the next succeeding place shall be divided evenly between the teams of the tied competitors.

6. In championship meets, team points will be awarded for the first 10 places as follows: 11 points for first place, 9 points for second, 8 points for third, and on down to 1 point for tenth place. The tie rule in dual competition also applies for championship meets.

7. In scoring AAU and intercollegiate competition, the judges shall award scores on the basis of 0 to 10 points with fractions of tenths of a point showing in the majority of cases. The 10 points are awarded as follows:

Difficulty	3.4 pts.
Composition	1.6 pts.
Execution	5.0 pts.

8. Four judges shall be used for each event. The scorekeepers for the meet shall take down each judge's score and strike out the highest and the lowest of the four scores and average the two middle scores. For example, a routine which has been evaluated by the judges as 9.60–9.50–9.40–9.30 would average as 9.45. When two identical high marks or low marks are recorded, only one will be discarded.

9. Points are to be deducted from the score if a spotter touches the performer during the exercise.

10. The meet referee is responsible for seeing that apparatus conforms to all specifications, acting as an authority in case of a dispute between judges, and insuring that all rules and regulations are enforced.

11. In the case of a defect in apparatus, the performer shall be allowed another trial.

12. The duration of a hold position (or balance) is three seconds. The penalty for intended positions held less than three seconds is $2/10$ to $4/10$ points.

13. If an exercise is not completed as a result of a fall from the apparatus, the maximum score which could be given is as follows:

$3/4$ of exercise completed	7.5 pts.
$1/2$ of exercise completed	5.0 pts.
$1/4$ of exercise completed	2.5 pts.

14. If a compulsory exercise is required, the gymnast may repeat it; however, only his repeat performance will be scored. A compulsory free calisthenic exercise may not be repeated.

15. In the long-horse event, both the compulsory and the optional vaults may be repeated, and in each case, the better of the two scores will count.

16. A beatboard may be used to mount the parallel bars; it is an official part of the long-horse event.

17. The following deductions for faults in an exercise may serve as a guide for judges in evaluating a performance:

Poor rhythm (too fast or too slow)	$1/10$ to $3/10$ pts.
Unprescribed hesitations	$2/10$ to $3/10$ pts.
Pronounced interruptions (or more serious stops)	$5/10$ to $8/10$ pts.
Falling from an apparatus	1.0 point
Touching the side horse or parallel bars with feet or legs	$1/10$ to $2/10$ pts.
Touching the floor or mat with feet from the side horse or parallel bars	$5/10$ to $7/10$ pts.
Walking in a handstand	$1/10$ to $5/10$ pts.
Poor holding of head or feet	$1/10$ to $2/10$ pts.
Unprescribed separating or bending of legs	$1/10$ to $2/10$ pts.

Unprescribed dipping or bending of arms	$\frac{1}{10}$ to $\frac{2}{10}$ pts.
Bent arms in handstand	$\frac{1}{10}$ to $\frac{3}{10}$ pts.
Bent arms and touching ropes in rings	$\frac{3}{10}$ to $\frac{5}{10}$ pts.
Bent arms in cross position in rings	$\frac{1}{10}$ to $\frac{5}{10}$ pts.
Too long a run in free exercise	$\frac{1}{10}$ to $\frac{3}{10}$ pts.
Crossing the limiting line in free exercise	$\frac{1}{10}$ to $\frac{3}{10}$ pts.
Poor posture in starting or landing position	$\frac{1}{10}$ to $\frac{2}{10}$ pts.
Small steps or hops in the dismount	$\frac{1}{10}$ to $\frac{2}{10}$ pts.
Several steps or hops in the dismount	$\frac{2}{10}$ to $\frac{3}{10}$ pts.
Touching floor or mat with hands	$\frac{2}{10}$ to $\frac{3}{10}$ pts.
Falling on back, knees, or hands	$\frac{5}{10}$ to $\frac{6}{10}$ pts.
(On the dismounts, the penalty may be reduced for bold or risky dismounts to 2/10 points.)	
Unnecessary swings	$\frac{3}{10}$ pts.
Breaks in the swinging motion	$\frac{1}{10}$ to $\frac{3}{10}$ pts.
Touching the long horse with feet, knees, or seat	$\frac{1}{10}$ to 1.0 pts.
Position of body too low over horse	$\frac{1}{10}$ to 1.0 pts.
Failing to stretch the body before landing from the long horse	$\frac{1}{10}$ to $\frac{5}{10}$ pts.

18. An optional exercise cannot be repeated, except for the long-horse vault.
19. Apparatus events must consist of at least ten principal parts; four parts must be of considerable difficulty and one part must be of superior difficulty. The free exercise routine must have six difficult parts and one superior part.
20. The specifications and types of movements to be used for each event are given in chapter 3.

It should be pointed out that gymnastic rules change frequently; therefore, the rules presented in this chapter may be somewhat out-of-date before they reach the reader. However, they should be useful in providing the beginner with some understanding of competitive gymnastics. The reader should be aware that current rule books are available.[1] [2]

References:

[1] *Gymnastics Guide*. Amateur Athletic Union, 231 West 58th Street, New York, 1962–1963.

[2] *Boxing, Gymnastics Rules*. National Collegiate Athletic Association, Box 757, Grand Central Station, New York, 17, New York, 1963–1964.

3

The Description, Characteristics, and Values of Gymnastic Events

It has been noted that many questions are now being posed by students, school administrators, and the public in general as to the nature of gymnastic equipment, the utilization of it, and the values which might be derived from its uses. Many such questions were occasioned by the seemingly impossible feats of strength, balance, flexibility, and timing of gymnastic performers on television and in the movies. It is hoped that the following material will help answer some of the many questions.

FREE EXERCISE

The free exercise event for boys is performed in an open floor area (39 feet 4.44 inches by 39 feet 4.44 inches) without the use of tumbling mats or other pieces of equipment. However, it is permissible to cover the floor area with a carpet of soft felt $3/16$ of an inch thick and covered with a tightly stretched canvas. When the canvas-covered pad is not used, the limit lines of the open floor area are generally marked off with tape.

Free exercise or free calisthenics for boys is characterized by movements which combine the elements of strength, balance, flexibility, and superb timing into a smooth and harmonious pattern. While each routine should possess a certain degree of each of the above elements, it is interesting to see how a boy with exceptional strength will work his exercise in such a manner so as to emphasize this quality in contrast to another performer who uses less strength work, but capitalizes on his agile and intricate tumbling ability.

Theories of what constitutes an excellent routine are in a constant state of change; however, at the present time the performer should keep the above points in mind and plan his routine in such a manner that all areas of the floor are adequately covered without stepping out of the marked-off area, and that the routine is within a time limit of from one minute to a minute and a half.

Some of the values of free exercise are listed as follows:

1. It has great carry over value in that it does not require the use of equipment, and individual stunts can be performed in small open areas.
2. It contributes to the development of strength and endurance throughout the entire body since the legs as well as the upper body are brought into play.
3. It offers the opportunity to experiment in as yet unexplored areas of body movement, thereby providing for individual creativity.
4. The very nature of the activity demands a greater development in flexibility, balance, strength, timing, and rhythmical movement.
5. It is a suitable activity for students of all grade levels in schools and colleges.

SIDE HORSE

The side horse is easily recognized by its two wooden pommels and its leather covered body. This piece of adjustable equipment is supported by either two or four legs. A few of the official dimensions are listed as follows:

Height from top of mat to top of pommels	4 feet
Length	60 to 62 inches
Width	14 to 15 inches
Distance between pommels	17½ to 18 inches

The horse may be raised or lowered to suit the purposes of the teacher in classwork. The horse is divided into three sections. From a side, stand frontways as you face the horse; the section to the left is the neck, the middle section is the saddle, and the end section on the right is the croup.

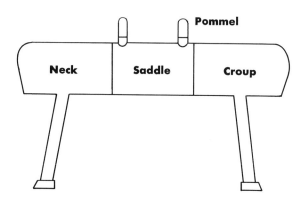

Side horse is a boys' event; it is characterized by a succession of swinging, turning, and vaulting movements that are executed without stopping or holding of position. In a well planned routine there is continuous motion along with changes in direction as all three sections of the horse are performed upon. It is generally considered the most difficult event in the gym to work, but also, the safest. Side-horse work though extremely challenging, nevertheless has a special appeal to students who have the ability to analyze and the patience to pursue a task for an extended period of time.

Some of the values of side-horse work are:

1. It offers some individuals with a limited kinesthetic sense an opportunity to excel, and those who are nearsighted are not at a disadvantage.
2. It provides an opportunity for some physically handicapped individuals to participate on an equal and sometimes better than equal basis. For example, those with lower limbs missing or those who are incapacitated from the waist down.
3. It contributes to the strengthening of the shoulders and arms.
4. In many instances, side-horse work requires the development of perseverance before mastery of a difficult stunt can be achieved.
5. It necessitates acquisition of a keen sense of timing along with rhythm, balance, and coordination.
6. It is a suitable activity for boys of all grade levels in junior high school, high school, and college.

PARALLEL BARS

The parallel bars is an adjustable piece of equipment consisting of two oval bars of equal height and equal length. Each bar is supported by two uprights attached to a heavy base. Although the bars may be raised, lowered, widened, or narrowed for classroom purposes, the dimensions for competition are listed as follows:

Height	63 to 67 inches
Width	16.53 to 18.89 inches
Length	11 feet and 6 inches

Parallel bars is an event for boys characterized by swinging and vaulting movements combined with a performance of strength and balance. A well-devised exercise should show precise timing in the swinging and vaulting movements which must predominate. Also, the exercise should travel at least the inside length of the bars showing release stunts above as well as below the bars with at least one change of direction. There must be at least one stunt displaying strength and not more than three hold positions.

A few of the values derived from participation on the parallel bars are listed as follows:

1. The student gains experience in making quick and accurate decisions.
2. It contributes to the development of upper-body strength.
3. The very nature of this activity demands the development of balance, strength, and precise timing.
4. It is a worthwhile activity for students of all grade levels in junior high school through college.

HORIZONTAL BAR

The horizontal bar is a polished steel bar supported by two metal uprights and four cables which are attached to floor plates. The dimensions of the most desirable type of horizontal bar are:

A bar that is 1.10 inches in diameter and 8 feet long.
A bar that can be adjusted in height from 3 feet to 8 feet 2 inches.

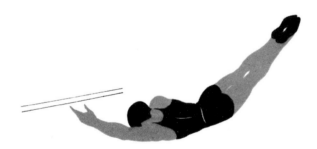

In competition the bar is about 8 feet from the floor; however, for class work, learning is usually best at about 4 to 5 feet.

Horizontal-bar work is characterized by swinging and vaulting movements performed in forward and backward directions without holding or stopping of positions. A well-planned routine should have a clever or surprising start and continue with stunts where direction is changed with a releasing and regrasping of the bar. The dismount should exhibit perfect control, and yet, should be performed in such a manner that it will draw a "gasp" from the spectators. In other words, the dismount should be of special value and daring in nature.

Some of the values of horizontal-bar work are:

1. It stimulates the development of the kinesthetic sense.
2. The courage and confidence of the circus acrobat are needed in performing high above the crowd.

3. It requires the development of split-second timing.

4. It is a valuable activity for boys in junior high school through college.

LONG HORSE

The long-horse event requires the use of the two following pieces of equipment:

1. The long horse which is the same as the side horse, except the pommels are removed. For competitive purposes, the height of the long horse is 53.15 inches measured from the floor to the top of the horse at the saddle.

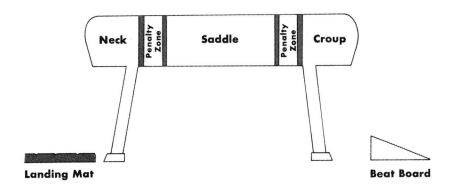

2. The beatboard which is a takeoff board, or springboard. Its dimensions are as follows:

Length	$47\frac{1}{4}$ inches
Height	$4\frac{3}{4}$ inches
Width	$23\frac{5}{8}$ inches

The long-horse event is characterized by a run with a double-foot takeoff from the beatboard in performing a vault lengthwise over the horse. All vaults must be executed with a momentary support of one or two hands as the performer passes over the horse. It is very important that the performer learns to make still landings. The distance of the run and the placement of the beatboard are left to the discretion of the gymnast. The performer may execute the same vault twice or two different vaults, with the better of the two scores counting.

The length of the long horse is divided into five sections. There are three sections each $15\frac{3}{4}$ inches long. These are the croup, saddle, and neck sections. The saddle is separated from the croup by a penalty zone of $7\frac{7}{8}$ inches and likewise, it is separated from the neck by a penalty zone of $7\frac{7}{8}$ inches. Thus, from the approach end of the horse (the end nearest the beatboard), the sections are listed in order as follows:

Croup	15¾ inches long
Penalty zone	7⅞ inches long
Saddle	15¾ inches long
Penalty zone	7⅞ inches long
Neck	15¾ inches long

The performer is penalized on cĕrtain vaults for each hand which touches the penalty zone.

A few of the values of long-horse vaulting are listed as follows:

1. It contributes to the development of leg power.
2. It teaches the individual to coordinate the legs and arms in clearing objects obstructing the path of flight.
3. It aids the development of timing and agility.
4. It encourages the development of courage and confidence.
5. It may be adjusted in height suitable to grade or age levels and is a desirable activity for boys in junior high school through college.

STILL RINGS

The still-rings event is conducted on wooden rings attached to adjustable straps which are in turn attached to ropes or cables hanging from a beam. For competitive purposes, the dimensions of the rings are as follows:

The two ropes or cables should hang from overhead fittings 18 feet from the floor. The rings should have a grip of 1.10 inches. The rings should be 18 inches apart and hang approximately 8 feet from the floor.

A still-rings exercise is characterized by combined movements of swing, strength, and holding of positions. At least two handstands must be held, one of which must be executed with strength, and the other with a swinging motion starting from or passing through a hanging position. Also, at least one position other than a handstand should be held with strength. The most impressive feature of still-rings work is the display of body strength and dynamics; the iron-cross is a must in top-flight competition.

Some of the values of still-rings work are listed as follows:

1. It contributes to the development of tremendous strength in the arms, chest, back, and the abdominal regions.
2. The very nature of this event requires the development of balance and rhythm.
3. Since most work on the rings requires primarily upper-body strength, it allows certain individuals handicapped from the waist down an opportunity to excel.
4. At present, skills are limited in this event; therefore, it offers an opportunity for the development of many new exercises.
5. This event is a desirable activity for boys of all grade levels in junior high school through college.

ALL-AROUND

To enter the all-around event, the competitor must compete in the six international or all-around events. These events are free exercise, long horse, side horse, parallel bars, horizontal bars, and still rings. The winner of the all-around event is the competitor who obtains the highest aggregate number of points from the six events listed above.

Some of the values derived from working the all-around events are listed as follows:

1. Working the all-around event encourages versatility.
2. It contributes to the development of strength throughout the entire body since the legs as well as the upper body are utilized in certain events.
3. It heightens adeptness of flexibility, balance, and exactness of movement.
4. The performer must learn to budget his time so that an equal amount can be spent on each event for a better all-around performance.

TUMBLING

The dimensions for the tumbling event are listed as follows:

Length of mats	60 feet
Width of mats	5 feet
Thickness of mats	2 to 4 inches

Tumbling is an event which is characterized by the performance of hand-springs and somersaults with twisting variations in rapid succession. In competition, the performer is expected to perform four routines down the mat within a two-minute time limit. The better performers normally show front and side tumbling which are advanced variations of the more common back tumbling stunts.

Some of the values of tumbling are listed as follows:

1. It strengthens the legs.
2. It contributes to the development of the kinesthetic sense.
3. Tumbling is not restricted to the use of mats or equipment. Most experienced tumblers can perform quite well whether executing their stunts outside on the grass or inside on the gym floor.
4. Tumbling skills have a great deal of carry-over value to other events in gymnastics as well as to other sports.
5. It is a worthwhile activity for all grade levels in elementary school, junior high school, senior high school, and college.

REBOUND TUMBLING

There are many models of rebound-tumbling apparatus; however, they all consist of a metal frame connected to a nylon or canvas bed by metal springs or elastic cords. The frame is usually covered by frame pads for protection. In the past, this piece of equipment was more commonly referred to as a trampoline.

For competitive purposes, the following dimensions are required:

The frame should be 17 by 10 feet
The bed should be 7 by 14 feet
The bed should be made of 1 inch nylon webbing.

Rebound tumbling is characterized by the performance of stunts in swing-time both forwards and backwards with a display of various twisting and rotating movements. In competition, the performer is allowed one routine which may include ten to twelve landings. At the beginning of the routine, the performer takes several preparatory bounces before performing the first stunt after which he may contact the bed ten to twelve times without rest.

Some of the values of rebound tumbling are listed as follows:

1. It develops a better sense of balance and relocation.
2. It contributes to the development of coordination and timing.
3. It strengthens the legs.
4. It encourages quick and accurate decisions.
5. It is a desirable and worthwhile activity for students of all grade levels in schools and colleges.
6. It is extremely appealing to spectators as well as being exciting for the performer.

SOCIAL VALUES

While considerable attention has been given to the contributions of gymnastics to the physical and motor development of the student, the social aspects of gymnastics are another important consideration. Gymnastics can also facilitate social adjustment through the following means:

1. By enabling all students to enjoy a rich social experience through a play and learning situation.
2. By encouraging students to work cooperatively with each other in spotting activities.
3. By teaching courtesy and concern for the welfare of others through the proper emphasis and observance of gymnastic safety rules.
4. By coordinating and unifying the personalities of students through the use of small informal groups which work together in the learning of stunts.

4

Gymnastic Warm-up and Strength-Development Exercises

GYMNASTIC WARM-UP EXERCISES

Just prior to engagement in the learning of stunts in the various gymnastic events, the beginner will find it beneficial to go through a light series of stretching exercises. These exercises are designed to increase flexibility and prepare the beginner for the more strenuous stunts ahead. The following exercises should be used at the beginning of each class or workout.

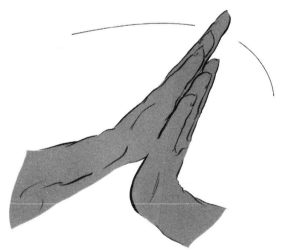

Wrist Warm-Ups

Place the palm of the right hand against the inward side of the fingers of the left hand and press them to the rear, causing an extension or stretching of the left wrist. After warming up the left wrist, perform the same movement against the right wrist. Wrist flexibility is extremely important for tumbling, balancing, and side-horse work.

Leg Extension Warm-Ups

With the feet slightly apart, lock the knees and bend downward, touching the floor with the fingers or palms of the hands for about ten repetitions. Leg extension in relation to the reach of the arms is especially important in free exercise and horizontal-bar work.

Splits

From a stand, extend the legs apart from front to rear or to opposite sides until the crotch is as near to the floor as possible. The splits increases flexibility for free-exercise movements, as well as for straddle vaults to and from apparatus.

Bridge-Ups

From a supine position on the floor, tilt the head back, arch the back, and walk the hands and feet as close together as possible. This exercise may also be executed by leaning backwards until contacting the wall and hand-walking down the wall until the hands and feet are on the floor. This exercise increases the flexibility of the back and shoulders which is important in tumbling and free exercise.

Shoulder Dislocates

Place the back to a bar, reach to the rear, and grasp the bar with a reverse grasp. Walk away from the bar until the shoulders roll or dislocate. Practice this movement striving to get the hands closer and closer together. This exercise develops shoulder flexibility which is necessary for rings and horizontal-bar stunts.

STRENGTH-DEVELOPMENT EXERCISES

Since gymnastics requires more upper-body strength than most sports, each class or workout should be followed by a short period of special exercises designed to develop strength.

Rope Climb

From a sitting position, climb hand over hand up a twenty foot rope. The beginner at first may have to use the feet, but, as his strength increases, he should use only the hands. This exercise is a good upper-body conditioner and increases the pulling power necessary for rings, parallel bars, and horizontal-bar work.

Handstand Push-Ups

Kick up into a handstand against a wall and bend at the elbows, allowing the body to lower until the nose or forehead touches the floor. Push the body back to its original position by extending the elbows until they lock. The beginner should strive to work up to at least ten repetitions prior to completing his basic course. This exercise develops the pressing power of the body which is necessary for free exercise, rings, and parallel bars.

Reverse and Regular Grasp Chin-Ups

The beginner should perform the reverse grasp chin-ups on one day and alternate using the regular grasp chin-ups the next day. The performer should strive to perform ten to twelve repetitions following each workout. This exercise develops the strength of the muscles across the front of the arms.

Dips

From a straight-arm support between the parallel bars, lower the body by bending the elbows until a steady resistance is met in the shoulders. Push the body back to a straight-arm support by extending the elbows until they lock. This exercise develops the strength of the triceps. Work up to ten to twelve repetitions.

Gymnastic Sit-Ups

From a supine position on a mat, bend at the waist raising the upper body and the legs to a piked position. When the hands touch the shins, return to a supine position. Work up to twenty or twenty-five repetitions. This exercise develops the strength of the abdominal muscles.

Isotonic Exercise

If the beginner finds the above exercises too easy, he should run a belt through a 5, 10, or 15 pound weight and attach this to his waist for added resistance. Isotonic (dynamic) contractions with barbells or dumbells are also beneficial in developing the strength or power necessary for certain gymnastic stunts.

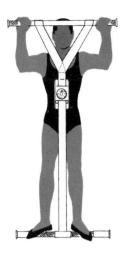

Isometric Exercise

Recent research in the field of strength development indicates that both isometric (static) and isotonic exercises are effective in promoting strength improvement. In a recent investigation by the writer, it was found that there was no significant difference between isometric and isotonic exercises concerning the improvement of velocity (speed) and distance in rope climbing.[1] An isometric scale and kit may be used quite effectively in measuring and developing strength for gymnastic activity.

EFFECTS OF REGULAR EXERCISE ON THE HUMAN BODY

Some of the effects of regular exercise (of a sufficient intensity and duration) on the human body that have been reported after careful experimentation are:

1. Improved cardiovascular endurance
2. Increased muscular strength
3. Increase in the size of muscle fibers
4. Increase in the number of capillaries in exercised muscles
5. Ability to obtain greater explosive power (an increase in force during initial movement) for the improvement of performance
6. Decrease in the formation of lactic acid resulting from exercise
7. A quicker return of pulse rate to normal following exercise
8. Improved mechanical efficiency
9. Removal, to some extent, of the inhibition to exert maximum effort in physical performance
10. Improved speed of movement and reaction time

HOME EXERCISES

In an evaluational study by Kenny,[2] it was found that exercising at home was the most popular form of maintaining physical fitness engaged in on an all-year basis among graduates from the University of Illinois. Since lack of time and facilities are limiting factors for many families, a quick workout at home represents the most practical approach to regular training or activity.

A number of exercises which may be executed within the limited space of most homes includes:

1. Gymnastic warm-up exercises (wrist warm-ups, leg extensions, splits, bridge-ups, and shoulder dislocates) as described in this chapter. The shoulder dislocates may be performed with a broom handle.

2. Strength development exercises (handstand push-ups against wall, gymnastic sit-ups, dips, and reverse and regular grasp chin-ups) as described in this chapter. The dips may be executed between two chairs and the chin-ups may be executed on the closet clothes bar by merely inserting a board with a notch in the upper end under the bar for added support. The knees and hips may be bent during the execution of such exercises when there is inadequate height between the floor and the point of support.

3. Balance stunts (tip-up, headstand, handstand, forearm balance, "L" balance, and scales) as described in Chapter 6.

4. Isometric exercises (numerous exercises may be performed within a limited space with an inexpensive isometric scale. Many such exercises have been described and illustrated by Drury.[3]

Developing a knowledge and appreciation of gymnastic skills and exercises in college will encourage their future use by students after they leave school.

References:

[1] Johnson, Barry L., *"A Comparison of Isometric and Isotonic Exercises Upon the Improvement of Velocity and Distance as Measured by a Vertical Rope Climb Test."* Louisiana State University, Baton Rouge, January, 1964. (unpublished study)

[2] Kenny, Harold E., "An Evaluative Study of the Required Physical Education Program for Men at the University of Illinois." *59th Annual Proceedings of the CPEA,* Urbana, 1956.

[3] Drury, Francis A., *Strength Through Measurement.* Marion, Ind., Coach's Sporting Goods Corporation, 1963.

5

Safety and Spotting Techniques

One of the major considerations in any gymnastic program is correct spotting and the close adherence to safety rules. The safety factor should be considered from the standpoint of facilities and equipment, the spotter, and the performer. While the principles and rules below are of a general nature, specific spotting techniques are presented directly following individual stunts in the succeeding chapters.

FACILITIES AND EQUIPMENT

1. When the gymnastics area is not under supervision, it should be locked from the rest of the building.
2. The gymnastic room should be large enough to allow a safe spacing of all equipment. The vertical clearance should be at least 20 feet. Minimum room size should be 50 feet by 80 feet.
3. All rebound tumbling equipment and other spring devices should be supervised when in use, or locked when not in use.
4. All ropes or cables should be checked periodically for excessive wear.
5. All attachments should be checked for tightness after each adjustment of the apparatus.
6. The hands should be protected from the wear and tear of excessive chalk deposits by sanding such deposits off the high bar, parallel bars, rings, and wooden pommels.
7. Equipment should be adjustable in order to facilitate the learning of new stunts at a low or safe level.
8. Climbing ropes should be carefully spaced so as to discourage students from swinging from one piece of equipment to another.

THE PERFORMER

1. Warm-up with light stretching exercises thoroughly before attempting harder stunts.
2. Learn fundamentals thoroughly before attempting advanced stunts.
3. Recognize the importance of the successful completion of each stunt and condition the body to meet this demand through flexibility or strength exercises.

Over-Head Spotting Rig

4. When necessary, learn stunts part by part and make use of available safety devices. (Research, however, supports learning stunts as functional wholes as more effective than by parts.)
5. Don't back out in the middle of a stunt, follow it through to completion.
6. Have confidence in your spotter and never use a spotter you can't trust.
7. Learn to perform with the eyes open throughout each stunt; this will enable you to make quick and accurate decisions when the need arises.
8. Learn to fall properly by employing the following principles:
   A. When possible, use the arms and legs to absorb the initial shock of landing. Upon contact with the floor, bend at the knees, elbows, and the waist.
   B. When possible, make use of a forward or backward rolling motion.
   C. When rolling forwards or when falling backwards, don't let the hands and arms get under the seat or back.
   D. When falling backwards, keep the chin tilted toward the chest and the arms by the sides with the fingers pointing forward. If possible, let the feet slap the floor before the seat, hands, and back contact.
9. Learn to judge the amount of exercise your hands can endure. Apparatus stunts are hard on the hands; therefore, they should be worked on gradually until the hands can withstand longer workouts.

10. Don't overwork tired muscles. Accidents are more likely to occur when the performer becomes physically tired.

THE SPOTTER

In gymnastics, a spotter is one who assists the performer from a safety standpoint. In gymnastic classes, students should learn how to spot as well as perform. Some of the rules for spotting are listed below:

1. Always know what the performer plans to do before you consent to spot for him.
2. Discuss with the performer the safest way for you to spot him.

The Hand-Spotting Technique

3. Don't overspot (give too much unnecessary assistance to) the performer. This can sometimes be as dangerous as failing to spot at all.
4. When possible, make use of other safety devices such as a handbelt, overhead safety rig, and protective mats, in addition to the hand spot.
5. When necessary, the spotter should center his support near the head and shoulders of the performer. This slows down the downward fall of the head and shoulders and allows the feet to reach the floor first.

Hand Spotting with Safety Belt

6. Do not catch, lift, or hold the performer unless necessary. Many times only a slight tap or touch is necessary for confidence.
7. Stay close to the performer but do not hinder or restrict the normal movements of the stunt.
8. Don't let your attention be distracted while the performer is in action.
9. Don't spot a performer unless you understand and know exactly what to do.

6

Free-exercise Stunts

The stunts presented in this chapter are frequently used in basic-tumbling and free-exercise routines. Many of the stunts are of a tumbling nature while others may be characterized as balance, flexibility, or strength stunts. The following stunts are not necessarily presented in a simple to complex sequence because of their varied nature. Concerning free-exercise stunts, it is felt by the writer that teacher and pupils should plan their own progression in accordance with their interests, needs, and abilities.

Forward Roll

From a position on the hands and knees, duck the head forward, push the hips over the head, and bend at the elbows, lowering the upper back to the mat while bending at the waist and the knees. As the upper back contacts the mat, grasp the shins with the hands and pull as *you roll down the back* and (from upper back to lower back) onto the buttocks and then onto the feet. When you have mastered the roll from the hands and knees, learn it from the squatting position and then from a full-standing position. If the back of the head or neck is allowed to contact the mat, it should be done in a gentle and controlled manner. Be sure and place your emphasis on learning one good forward roll and not a series of fast rolls executed with poor technique.

Safety: The performer should concentrate on keeping his body weight primarily on the hands and arms, while lowering gently onto the upper back during the roll.

Shoulder Roll

From a stand with the right leg a pace ahead of the left leg, bend forward looking between the legs and lower onto the right forearm. Push with the feet and roll over the right shoulder and diagonally across the back and onto the left hip. Keep the legs spread apart and as you roll onto the left hip, bend the left leg at the knee so that you roll onto the left knee, push with left hand, and step out on the right foot returning to a standing position. This stunt may be executed over either the left or right shoulder.

Dive Roll

Take several running steps and a low hurdle onto both feet, bounce from both feet, extend the arms, ride the hips high, and keep the head up until the hands contact the mat. As the hands contact the mat, bend the arms slowly while ducking the head and bending at the waist and knees. From this point, continue the roll to a standing position as described in the forward roll. The beginner's pike-dive roll is illustrated, but an arch dive might be learned eventually.

Safety: Use double thickness mats while learning and avoid contact with the head or neck unless such contact can be carefully controlled.

Tip-Up

From a squatting position, place the hands shoulder width apart with the fingers pointing straight ahead. Lean forward bending at the elbows and place the inside of the knees against and slightly above the outside of the elbows. Continue to lean forward until the feet come off of the floor and balance on both hands with the face several inches from the floor.

Safety: If the performer overbalances forward, he should duck the head and perform a forward roll.

Backward Roll

From a sitting position, the performer rolls backward onto the upper back placing the hands on the mat with the thumbs next to the ears while keeping the legs straight and the waist flexed. As the body weight is shifted onto the hands, the performer pushes with the arms, looks upward with the head, and extends the hips into an arched position. Passing through a momentary handstand, the performer may either snap down to the feet or step down one foot at a time.

Safety: For the first few trials a spotter should kneel on both knees next to the performer's left shoulder, cupping the fingers of the right hand from the performer's back to a position over the top of the shoulders. The left hand is placed in the small of the performer's back and as the performer rolls backward and begins the push with the arms, the spotter lifts and assists the performer through the momentary hand balance. A spotter may be used to either side.

Headstand

From a stand, bend forward, placing the hands on the mat shoulder width apart with fingers pointing straight ahead. Place the forehead on the mat several inches ahead of the hands. Keeping the body weight primarily on the hands, kick upward one foot at a time and maintain your balance with the back slightly arched, legs straight and together, and toes pointed. In placing the head on the mat, do not use the top of the head. The hairline usually serves as a good guide as to where to place the forehead. To get out of this position, push with the hands, duck the head, and roll forward, or step down on one foot at a time.

Safety: As the performer kicks upward, the spotter should be standing to the side and slightly to the rear in order to grasp the performer's legs and assist them in the proper position on the first few trials.

Cartwheel

From a stand with the legs a pace apart, raise the arms horizontally to the sides and shift the weight to the right, lifting the left foot slightly off of the ground. As you shift the weight back to the left side, bend at the waist and place the left hand about a pace away from the left foot. As the left hand moves to the mat, the right leg is raised and at the point of contact of the left hand to the mat, the left foot pushes from the floor. As the momentum carries the body weight onto the left arm, reach about shoulder width apart with the right arm so that the body weight is momentarily on both arms. At this point, the performer's position is a handstand with the head up and looking forward ahead of the hands. The back is slightly arched and the legs are straight and stretched wide apart. As the right hand contacts the mat, push with the left hand, then push with the right hand and bend at the waist, stepping down on the right foot. As the right foot comes to the mat, stretch the left leg and step down onto the left foot so that it is a pace away from the right foot. This should place the performer in the same direction and approximate stance that he was in at the beginning of the stunt. This stunt may be executed to the left or right.

Safety: A spotter may stand directly behind the performer and place his right hand on the performer's left hip and cross the left arm over so that the left hand is on the performer's right hip. As the performer moves to the left, the spotter moves with him, lifting and assisting the performer through the correct position.

Forearm Balance

From a kneeling position on one knee and one foot, place the forearms on the mat with the fingers straight ahead and slightly flexed. Kick upward one foot at a time and maintain a balanced position with feet overhead and with the head up and looking between the hands. The back should be slightly arched, legs straight and together, and the toes pointed. To get out of this position, duck the head and roll forward or bend at the waist and step downward one foot at a time.

Safety: Same as for the headstand.

Cartwheel and Quarter Turn

This stunt is performed in the same manner as the cartwheel, except that as the right foot contacts the mat, the performer stretches the left leg and both arms while making a quarter turn on the ball of the right foot. As he makes the turn, the left foot steps out a pace, placing the performer in a good position to go into another stunt.

Safety: Same as for the cartwheel.

Handstand

From a stand, bend forward and place the hands on the floor about shoulder width apart. The fingers should be spread apart and slightly flexed with the fingertips pressed against the floor and pointed straight ahead. Lean the shoulders over the hands and separate the feet so that one foot is ahead of the other. The head should be held up so that the eyes are looking forward of the fingertips. Swing the rear foot upward as you kick or push the near foot from the floor and maintain a balanced position with the feet overhead. This position should be maintained several seconds with the back straight or slightly arched, legs straight and together, and toes pointed.

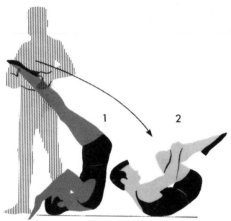

A. There are several methods used to get out of this position. They are described as follows:

1. Step downward one foot at a time to the rear.
2. Overlean forward keeping the right hand in place and turn the head and shoulders to the right, causing the body to turn. The performer then merely separates the legs and steps down one foot at a time. The spotter should stand on the right side and place the right hand on the performer's left hip and the left hand on the right hip and turn the performer to the right.
3. Bend the elbows slowly, duck the head, and perform a forward roll back to the feet. In this method the spotter should grasp the ankles and lift them gently as the performer rolls forward. The spotter should release his grasp as the performer's back contacts the mat.

B. There are also several methods used to learn the handstand. They are described as follows:

Spotter and Wall Method

1. Place the hands about a normal step away from a wall and kick upward into a handstand with the assistance of a spotter. The distance from the wall will vary according to the individual. The spotter should assume a position to the side of the performer with one hand grasping the near shoulder and the other hand grasping the performer's near leg just above the knee. When the performer is secure against the wall, the spotter may remove his hand from the shoulder and use both hands in assisting the performer to maintain a free balance between the wall and the spotter's

hands. The performer should avoid ducking the head since it could cause him to roll into the wall. The spotter and wall method is most often used to get the beginner started on the handstand.

Spotter Method

In this method, the spotter stands directly to the side of the performer and grasps his legs as he kicks upward. When the performer is in the handstand position, the spotter releases his grasps on the legs and places one arm in front of the shins and the other arm behind the legs, allowing the performer to maintain a free balance without letting him completely overbalance to the front or the rear.

Unassisted Method

This method is most commonly used when the performer has suc-

ceeded in learning how to kick upward into position, hesitate, and get out of position safely. In this method, the performer works without assistance in attempting to maintain his balance on the hands. He learns to check or correct his balance by raising the head and pressing with the fingertips, shifting the body weight slightly to the rear when he is overbalancing forward; and to lower the head and lean the shoulders slightly forward, causing the body weight to shift toward the fingers when he is overbalancing to the rear. Learning the handstand takes some individuals much longer than others; however, the fastest way to develop a good handstand is to spend at least fifteen minutes a day working on it until you can consistently maintain this position for 3 or 4 seconds.

Kip-Up

From a sitting position, roll backward piking at the hips and keeping the legs straight. Place the hands on the mat with the thumbs next to the ears and let the body weight rest on the hands and upper back. Hesitate when the knees come directly over the face and then immediately push with the hands and lash the legs upward, outward, and then downward. This action should cause the head and shoulders to rise, allowing the performer to land in a standing position.

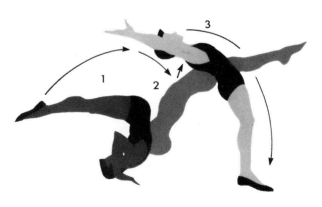

Safety: This stunt can be taught on the trampoline or by the use of a spotter. The spotter should position himself to the side of the head and shoulders of the performer. If spotting on the right side, the spotter places the right hand

on the performer's neck and the left hand at the small of the back. When the performer lashes upward and outward, the spotter lifts and assists him to the feet.

Forward Roll to Straddle Stand

From a stand, perform a forward roll and as the body weight gets on the upper back, split the legs wide apart and rush the roll onto the seat; driving the heels of the feet into the mat with force. As soon as the legs split, place the hands on the mat between the legs and as close to the crotch as possible. As the momentum from the roll carries you up onto your feet, push with the hands and lean the head and shoulders well forward. The legs should be kept straight throughout and the performer should complete the stunt in a wide-straddle stand or splits.

Headspring

Run forward on the mat, lift the left foot from the floor, and skip on the right foot. After skipping on the right foot, place the left foot on the mat, bend at the waist, and place the hands a pace ahead of the left foot while bending at the elbows and placing the top of the head a few inches in front of the hands. Swing the right leg upward while pushing forcefully with the left foot. As the legs come upward toward the headstand position, pike at the hips and as the hips overlean forward, push with the hands and extend the legs from the hips upward, out-

ward, and downward. As the head and shoulders rise, the performer may land on the feet with the back arched and legs straight, or with knees and hips slightly bent. This stunt is commonly executed from a double-foot takeoff.

Safety: This stunt should be learned from the rolled mat and with the assistance of a spotter. Spotting on the right side of the mat, the spotter places the left knee on the edge of the rolled mat and stretches the right leg forward on the edge of the landing mat. The spotter grasps the performer's right wrist with the left hand and as the performer turns upside down, he places the right hand under the small of the back and assists the performer to his feet.

Handspring

Run forward on the mat and lift the left foot from the floor and skip on the right foot. After skipping on the right foot, place the left foot on the mat, bend at the waist, and place the hands a pace ahead of the left foot while keeping the arms straight and the eyes looking forward of the hands. Swing the right leg upward while pushing forcefully with the left foot. As the legs move upward through the handstand position, extend the shoulders and push with the hands and fingers. The back should be arched and as the head and shoulders rise, the performer should land on both feet with the legs straight or slightly bent, and the feet either even or separated into a walk-out position.

Safety: Same as for the headspring.

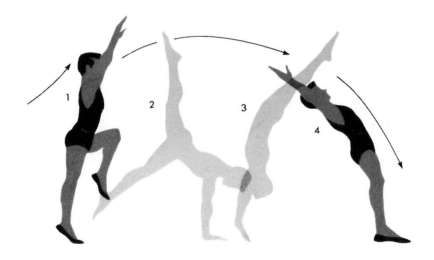

"L" Position on Hands

From a sitting position on the floor, place the hands close to the sides of the hips and on the floor. Push with the hands by extending the shoulders, and lift the legs and seat from the floor. Keep the head up, chest out, legs straight, toes pointed, arms straight, and hold for several seconds. Some performers find it easier to slowly roll from the back forward onto the hands without letting the hips or legs touch the floor.

Front Scale

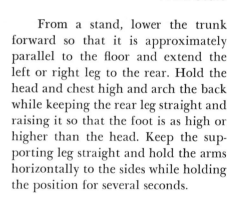

From a stand, lower the trunk forward so that it is approximately parallel to the floor and extend the left or right leg to the rear. Hold the head and chest high and arch the back while keeping the rear leg straight and raising it so that the foot is as high or higher than the head. Keep the supporting leg straight and hold the arms horizontally to the sides while holding the position for several seconds.

Side Scale

From a standing position, lean to the left side and lift the right leg until it is horizontal to the floor. The left arm is extended to the left and horizontal to the floor while the right arm is extended along the right side of the body with the hand resting on the thigh. The head may be held in its natural arc or it may be leaned close to the extended left arm. The supporting leg should be kept straight while maintaining the position for several seconds.

Front Splits

From a stand, slide the left or right foot forward, lowering the body downward until the crotch is within an inch of the floor. With one leg extended to the front and the other leg extended to the rear, maintain the splits position with the toes pointed, head up, and arm spread horizontally to the sides.

Side Splits

From a stand, slide the feet apart and to the sides lowering the body downward until the crotch is within an inch of the floor. The upper body faces forward and may be held upright or parallel to the floor. The arms should be extended horizontally to the sides.

Routine

Each student should be encouraged to create a free-exercise or tumbling routine using as many of the above stunts as possible.

PHYSICAL PRINCIPLES INVOLVED IN FREE EXERCISE

A few of the scientific principles involved in executing free exercise stunts are listed as follows:

1. Static balance is directly proportional to the area of the base on which the body is supported.

Example: Greater stability is gained in the handstand position if the fingers are spread well apart.

2. In support stunts, the center of gravity of the body should fall as nearly as possible over the point of support (the hands, arms, or feet).

> **Example:** In the "L" position on the hands, the center of gravity falls at a point directly between the hands.

3. A body may be put into motion by the transfer of momentum from a body part to the whole.

> **Example:** In the kip-up on a mat, the legs lash out and down, causing the body to rise to an upright position.

4. To absorb the shock of a fall, the shock should be spread over as large an area as possible and as long a distance as possible.

> **Example:** If a headspring or handspring is overturned, the performer should extend the arms, wrists, and fingers and relax gradually giving-in upon contact with the mat (spreading out the shock) rather than landing on the face or chest.

5. For every force there is always an equal and opposite counterforce.

> **Example:** In executing the back roll, the hands push against the mat after the center of gravity passes the point of support. The reaction from the push, turns and lifts the body to a standing position.

6. In pressing body weight, the center of gravity should fall as nearly as possible over the point of support. This reduces the effort necessary to raise the body.

> **Example:** In pressing from a tip-up to a handstand, get the hips over the hands as early as possible in the press.

7. A body will turn faster when the length of the radius of rotation about the center of gravity is decreased.

> **Example:** A performer turns faster from a dive roll by tucking the knees and waist after he contacts the mat with the hands and upper back.

Side-horse Stunts

The following stunts for side horse are presented in a simple to complex progression. However, it should be noted that this particular sequence is arbitrary and is not meant to be inflexible. After assessing his individual interests and capabilities, the reader will be able to form his own order of learning.

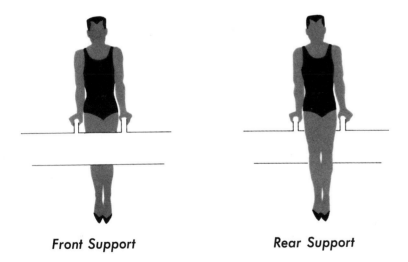

Front Support   *Rear Support*

Straddle Slide

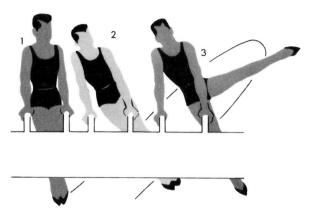

From a front-support position with straight arms, lean on the right arm and swing both legs to the left, sliding the legs along the side of the horse. As the legs reach the peak of their swing, allow them to separate, causing the left leg to rise high above the horse. As the legs swing back, lean on the left hand and allow the legs to perform the same movement to the right. Perform this movement several times in succession to warm up the wrists and develop rhythm and proper lean.

Squat Mount to "L"

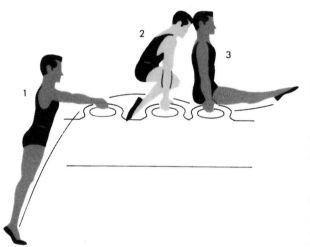

Grasp the pomels with both hands and jump the hips upward while extending the arms and shoulders and leaning forward. Bend at the knees and waist and pass the legs between the arms and over the saddle to a straight-leg bent-body "L" position. Hold this position for several seconds with the head up, legs horizontal to the floor, and toes pointed. Holding this position should contribute to the development of abdominal strength which is necessary for successful side-horse performance.

Feint Swings

From a front-support position with straight arms, shift the body weight on the right arm as you swing the right leg over the right end of the horse, thus straddling the right arm with the legs. From this position, swing the right leg back to the starting position, shifting the weight to both arms. Then lean on the left arm, and continue the left leg over the left end of the horse, straddling the left arm. Perform this movement several times to warm up the wrists, develop momentum, and improve proper lean.

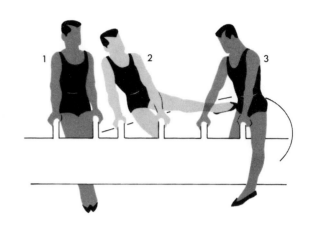

Single-Leg Half-Circles

From a front-support position with straight arms, swing the right leg over the right end of the horse while leaning on the left arm. As the weight is shifted to the left arm, the right leg passes under the right hand and over the right pommel to a position between the pommels. The weight is then shifted to the right arm as the left leg performs the same movement over the left end of the horse between and under the left hand to join the right leg in the center of the horse. As each leg passes under each hand, remember to regrasp, keeping the arms straight. Return to the starting position by swinging the right leg under the right hand and the left leg under the left hand, finishing in a straight-arm front support.

Single-Leg Full-Circle

From a front-support position with straight arms, lean to the right and swing the left leg over the left end of the horse. Release with the left hand and pass the left leg over the left pommel into the center. Regrasp with the left hand on the left pommel and lean to the left as the left leg continues its swing under the right hand and over the right end of the horse. Regrasp with the right hand as you return to the original position with straight arms. While the left leg is the center of attention as described above, the right leg remains on the approach side of the horse swinging to the left with the left leg, but returning to the right as the left leg cuts over the horse and continues to the right. This stunt may be performed to the left or right.

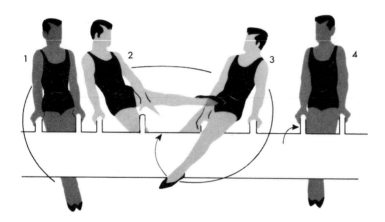

Double-Leg Half-Circles

From a feint position around the right arm, swing the legs to the left, passing them over the horse and between the left hand and the pommel. Regrasp with the left hand, keeping the arms straight, and stop in a straight-arm rear support. From this position, lean to the left and swing the

legs over the right pommel and under the right hand, returning them to the approach side of the horse. As the legs clear the right pommel, regrasp with the right hand and return to a straight-arm front-support position. This stunt may be performed to the left or right.

A helpful hint to note in executing this stunt is that as the regrasp is made with the right hand, lean slightly forward with the right shoulder and keep the right arm straight; otherwise, the performer will not be able to finish in a straight-arm front support.

Double-Leg Half-Cut Mount to Single-Leg Half-Circles

From a stand with the hands on the pommels, jump while leaning on the right arm and cut both legs between the left hand and left pommel. As the left hand regrasps the left pom-mel, lean on the left arm and cut the right leg between the right hand and and right pommel. As the right hand regrasps the right pommel, perform the same movement to the left with the left leg. The stunt is completed with the performer in a straight-arm front-rest position. This stunt may be performed to the left or right.

Single-Rear Dismount

From a front support with the left hand on the neck of the horse and the right hand on the left pommel, feint around the right arm. From this position, lean on the right arm and swing the legs over the left end of the horse and under the left hand. With the left hand regrasp the end of the horse, release with the right hand, and land on both feet with the left side nearest to the neck of the horse. On the landing, the right arm should be extended horizontally to the side. This stunt may be performed to the left or right.

Single-Leg Travel

From a front-support position on the pommels with straight arms, swing the right leg over the right end of the horse while leaning on the left arm. With the weight on the left arm, the right leg passes under the right hand and over the right pommel to a position between the pommels. The weight is then shifted to the right arm as the

left leg swings over the left end of the horse. The body weight is then shifted back to the left arm as the left leg comes to rest next to the left hand and left pommel. The performer's legs are at this point straddling the left hand and left pommel. As the right leg swings between the right hand and right pommel in order to move over the right end of the horse, the right hand is shifted to the left pommel and in front of the left hand. As the right leg clears the right end of the horse, the left leg swings back over the left end of the horse and the left hand is shifted to the end of the neck section. This stunt may be executed to the left or right.

Double-Rear Dismount

With the hands on the pommels, attain a feint position with the legs straddling around the right arm. Keeping the body weight on the right arm, swing the right leg around the croup so that it joins the left leg and lift the left hand from the left pommel so that the legs can swing over the pommel and continue toward the croup. The head, shoulders, and hips should turn to the right so that when the legs clear the end of the croup, the left hand can rest on the end of the croup. At this point the right hand is released from the right pommel, the feet land on the mat with the left side closest to the croup, and the right arm is extended horizontally to the side. This stunt may be performed to the left or right.

Safety: As the performer's right leg joins the left leg from the feint position, a spotter may step in and grasp the right wrist with the right hand and the left hip with the left hand and thus assist the clearing of the end of the horse as well as the landing.

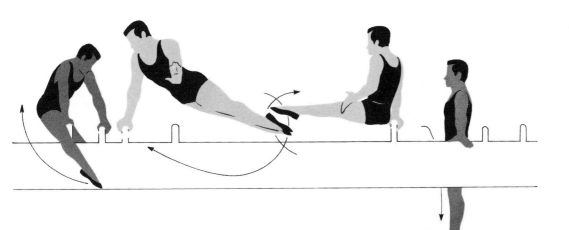

Front Scissors

From a straight-arm support with the right leg between the pommels and in front of the horse and the left leg in back of the horse, swing the legs to the left as you lean on the right arm. When the legs near the peak of their swing, release with the left hand and cross the right leg under the left leg. As the legs cross, they separate and return downward with the left leg to the front and between the pommels and the right leg to the back. The left hand regrasps as soon as the crotch passes between the pommels. This stunt may be executed to the left or right.

Safety: For the first few trials, the performer should place the feet on the left end of the horse with the left hand still between the legs and on the pommel. As the performer slides the right leg under the left leg, he should release with the left hand, complete the scissors of the legs, and regrasp as the crotch passes into the center between the pommels. This method instills confidence and thereby facilitates the process of learning the scissors.

Rear Scissors

From a straight-arm support with the left leg between the pommels and to the front and the right leg in back of the horse, swing the legs to the left and lean on the right arm. When the legs near the peak of their swing, release with the left hand and cross the right leg under the left leg. As the legs cross, they separate and return downward with the right leg to the front and between the pommels and the left leg to the rear. The left hand regrasps as soon as the crotch passes between the pommels. The stunt may be performed to the left or right.

Safety: For the first few trials, the performer should place the feet on the left end of the horse with the left hand still between the legs and on the pommel. As the performer slides the right leg under the left leg, he should release with the left hand, complete the scissors of the legs, and regrasp as the crotch passes into the center of the pommels.

Beginner's Baby Moore

Grasp the pommels and jump the right leg between the arms and over the saddle. From this position, swing the left leg over the left end of the horse, shifting the body weight onto the left hand. Release the right hand from the right pommel as the right leg passes over the pommel and place the right hand in a reverse grasp alongside the left hand on the left pommel. Keep the right leg moving to the right in a wide arc and lean on the right hand, releasing the left hand and grasping the pommel to the left. As the right leg clears the end of the horse, the performer should be facing the opposite direction from which he started. This stunt may be executed to the left or right.

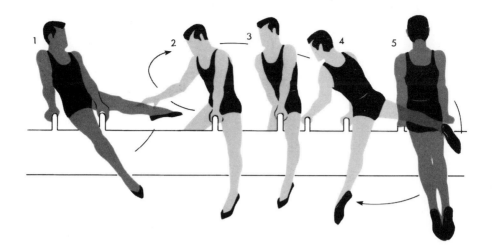

Baby-Loop Mount

From a stand facing the end of the neck section of the horse, place the left hand on the end and left side of the neck and the right hand on the end and right side of the neck. Keeping the body weight on the right hand, jump (lifting and swinging) the legs over the pommels. The head, shoulders, and hips should turn to the right as the legs go up and over the pommels. The left hand should grasp the near pommel as the legs clear it and the right hand should remain on the end of the neck section. The stunt is completed in a rear-support position with both legs between the left and

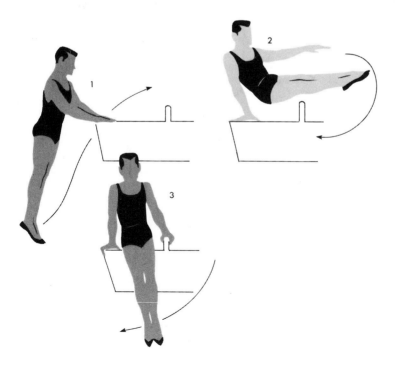

the right hand. As the performer be-comes more adept, he should strive to start the mount from a position facing the neck section with the right hand on the left pommel and the left hand on the end of the neck.

Safety: A spotter may stand behind the performer grasping his belt with the left hand and placing the right palm under the right buttocks. As the performer jumps, the spotter lifts, turns, and assists the performer into the completed position.

Hop-Turn Travel (From Saddle to Croup)

From a straddle support in the saddle, with the right leg in front and the left leg in the rear, lean on the right arm as the left leg cuts under the left hand. As this cutting action takes place, press the back of the right leg against the saddle and hop to the end section of the horse. While execut-ing the hop, both legs should come together and the lean should continue to the right until the legs have passed over the end of the horse. The stunt is completed with the left hand on the end section, the right hand still on the pommel, and the legs between the hands. The stunt may be performed to the left or right.

Safety: From a position facing the performer, a spotter may step for-ward and give assistance after the legs of the performer meet and start toward the croup.

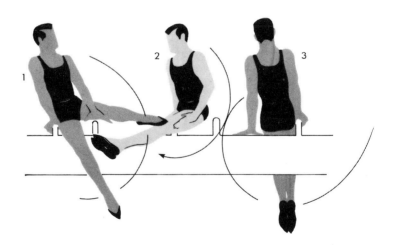

Routine

Combine five or six stunts into a routine which is in some way differ-ent from the routines of other mem-bers of the class.

PHYSICAL PRINCIPLES INVOLVED IN SIDE-HORSE WORK

A few of the scientific principles involved in executing side-horse stunts are listed as follows:

1. The center of gravity of the body should fall as nearly as possible over the point of support.

> **Example:** In side-horse stunts, the center of gravity is held over the hands by leaning the shoulders in one direction as the hips move in the opposite direction.

2. Twisting movements which are started while the body is on a rotating support will be in the direction of the movement of those parts of the body which are used to initiate it.

> **Example:** In executing the hop-turn travel to the right, the rotating support is the right arm and the twist to the right is caused by turning the head, shoulders, and hips to the right.

3. The center of gravity must always be moved first in the direction where movement is desired.

> **Example:** In performing single-leg half circles, the center of gravity is first shifted to the right in order to cut the left leg between the left hand and left pommel so that it can move to the right.

4. The shift of the center of support is always made when the body is at the peak of its swing.

> **Example:** This is evident in shifting the left hand from the left pommel to the left end of the horse in a single-leg travel.

5. For every force there is always an equal and opposite counterforce.

> **Example:** In initiating a single-leg full-circle, the action of the shoulders leaning to the right causes the reaction of the legs moving to the left.

6. In swinging stunts, decreasing the radius of rotation (distance between the center of gravity and the center of rotation) on the swing upward will accelerate the movement.

> **Example:** In executing double-leg half-circles, piking at the hips as the legs swing between the right hand and right pommel (moving from a rear support to a front support) facilitates the clearing of the end of the horse and accelerates the movement.

8

Vaulting Stunts

VAULTING TECHNIQUE

The beginner should learn to take a short, low hurdle on the beatboard from an abbreviated run before attempting any of the vaults below. The hurdle should not be used to get height, but merely to get both feet on the beatboard at the same time. In order to attain a reasonable amount of consistency, the performer should start from a predetermined distance measured from a desired spot on the beatboard. The performer should run fast enough to attain the necessary speed to perform the vault without sacrificing control. The eyes should be fixed on the beatboard at the start of the run and should remain there until a few feet before the hurdle is executed. Just prior to making the hurdle, the eyes should shift to the spot on the horse that the performer wishes to contact with the hands. The hurdle is made by jumping off one foot and landing both feet on the beatboard at the same time. The landing on the beatboard should be made on the balls of the feet, avoid landing flat-footed. The placing of the beatboard and the angle of the takeoff from it varies in accordance with the performer's physique and with the type of vault being executed. Following the desired vault over the horse, the performer should land on both feet with the knees bending naturally as the feet contact the mat and with the arms extending horizontally to the sides. Avoid taking extra hops or steps after the feet contact the mat.

SIDE-HORSE VAULTING

While side-horse vaulting (without pommels) is a competitive event for women, it is of the utmost importance in the teaching of vaulting to beginning male students in gymnastics. The beginner may profit from learning side-horse vaults and fundamentals of long-horse vaulting through the use of the side horse (with or without pommels). The following stunts are presented with the use of the pommels in mind. However, the pommels may be removed and the horse may be raised or lowered as the needs of the group or individual so indicate.

Squat Vault

Run forward, take off from the beatboard with both feet, and reach for the pommels. As the hands contact the pommels, bend at the waist and knees and push and release with the hands while the legs pass between the arms in a squat position. As the push is made, raise the head upward and stretch the body prior to the landing. The landing should be made on both feet with the back to the horse.

Safety: One or two spotters may stand on the landing side of the horse and grasp the near arm as the performer executes his release.

Front Vault

Run forward and take off from the beatboard with both feet. Grasp the pommels and turn the head and shoulders to the right while allowing the hips to rise and the legs to pass over the left end of the horse. The body weight should be on the right arm as the front of the body turns and faces the horse with the back arched. The left hand is released from the left pommel prior to the legs passing over the left end of the horse and is extended to the side as the performer lands on both feet with the right side nearest the horse. This vault may be performed to the left or right.

Safety: For those beginners who are hesitant to perform this stunt in the middle, move the beatboard to the neck section of the horse so that the beginner's legs pass over and beyond the end of the horse. Stress leaning on the right arm.

Flank Vault

Run forward and take off from the beatboard with both feet. Grasp the pommels with both hands and lean on the right arm as you turn the right side of the body toward the horse. Release with the left hand and carry the legs over the left end of the horse. Release with the right hand and land on both feet with the back to the horse and the arms extended to the sides. This vault may be performed to the left or right.

Safety: Standing on the landing side of the horse, the spotter grasps the right wrist of the performer and assists him to his feet, if necessary. This stunt may also be performed over the neck end of the horse.

Rear Vault

Run forward and take off from the beatboard with both feet. Grasp the pommels with both hands and as the hips rise, lean on the right arm and release the left hand as the legs pass over the left pommel and under the left hand. When the legs pass over the left pommel, regrasp with the left hand, release with the right hand, and land with the left side nearest the horse and the right arm extended horizontally to the side. This vault may be executed left to right.

Safety: Same as for the flank vault.

Straddle Vault

Run forward and take off from the beatboard with both feet. Grasp the pommels with both hands and as the hips rise, lean on the hands, split the legs wide, pike at the waist, push with the hands, and release. Keep the head up as the feet clear the ends of the horse. When the feet clear the horse, stretch the body, close the legs, and land on both feet with the back to the horse.

Safety: If possible, use two spotters on the landing side of the horse. As the performer releases with the hands, the spotters should reach forward and grasp the performer's arms and assist him to the feet.

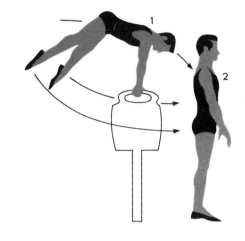

Stoop Vault

Run forward and take off from the beatboard with both feet. Grasp the pommels with both hands and as the hips rise, lean forward on the hands, pike at the waist, push and release with the hands, and snap the legs between the pommels while maintaining a straight-leg position. As the feet clear the saddle of the horse, raise the head, chest, and arms (stretching) and land on both feet with the back to the horse.

Safety: Same as for the straddle vault.

Thief Vault

Run forward taking off from the beatboard one foot at a time. Lift the leg up and through the pommels while pushing from the right leg. Immediately following this motion, draw the right leg between the pommels so that it joins the left leg. At this point, the legs are ahead of the body. As the hips rise over the pommels, place the hands on the pommels and give a quick push so that the head and chest will lift upward for the landing.

Safety: A spotter should stand to the side of the point of landing and be ready to assist the performer if the need arises.

Neckspring Vault

Run forward and take off on both feet while grasping the pommels with the hands. Pike at the waist and carry the hips high over the pommels. As the hips rise, the arms should bend and the head should be ducked under so that the back of the neck gently contacts the saddle of the horse. As the hips overlean toward the landing area, forcefully extend the legs forward (out of the pike position) and push and release with the hands. The landing should be made upon both feet while bending slightly at the knees and waist, and extending the arms horizontally to the sides.

Safety: Standing on the landing side and to the left of the performer, the spotter should grasp the left wrist while the performer's hand is on the pommel and use the right hand to assist in speeding up or slowing down the landing of the performer. The first few attempts at this stunt may be performed from a kneeling position on the horse or from a standing spring off of the beatboard.

Headspring Vault

The headspring vault is performed in the same manner as the neckspring vault, except that the top of the head gently contacts the saddle instead of the back of the neck. In this stunt, the arms must exert a little more effort than in the neckspring.

Safety: Same as for the neckspring.

Handspring

The handspring vault is performed in the same manner as the headspring vault, except that the head does not touch the saddle. Also, there must be a greater effort on the part of the legs in taking off from the beatboard so that the legs and hips will rise high above the extended arms and still have enough speed to overturn for the landing. While most beginners will bend at the elbows and hips, they should continually strive to pass through a handstand position.

Safety: Same as for the neckspring and headspring. This stunt may also be learned by placing the side horse next to the end of the trampoline and draping a mat from the trampoline across the springs and the side horse (without pommels). The spotter may then assist from the approach side of the horse.

LONG-HORSE VAULTING

While there are numerous vaults that can be performed on the long horse, the author considers most of them too difficult for the beginning student in gymnastics. However, with the horse set at a low level, the beginner should be able to lay a foundation for performing more advanced vaults by learning to perform the less complex stunts presented below.

Stand on Croup and Straddle from Neck

From a stand on the croup, jump the hips and feet upward three-quarters of the way to a handstand while placing the hands on the neck of the horse. Push vigorously with the hands and snap down with the legs separating. When the push with the hands has been completed, raise the head and arms as the hips straighten and focus the eyes on the landing area during the descent.

Safety: If possible, use two spotters on the sides of the landing area. As the performer releases with the hands, the spotters should reach forward and grasp the performer's arms and assist him to the feet. Lower the horse as much as necessary while learning.

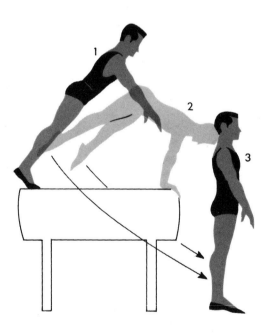

Stand on Croup and Squat from Neck

From a stand on the croup, jump the hips and feet upward three-quarters of the way to a handstand while placing the hands on the neck of the horse. Push vigorously with the hands and snap downward, bending at the knees and the waist. When the push with the hands has been completed, raise the head and arms as the hips and legs straighten and focus the eyes on the landing area during the descent. The feet and knees should press together throughout the stunt.

Safety: Same as for the stand on croup and straddle from neck.

Straddle from Neck

Run forward and while taking off from the balls of the feet, cause the feet and hips to rise while reaching forward with the hands to the neck section of the horse. When the hands contact the horse and maximum height has been reached with the hips, push vigorously with the hands, separate the legs, and snap downward (stretching the body) to the landing area.

Safety: Same as for the stand on croup and straddle from neck.

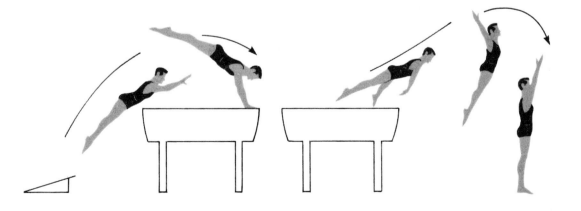

Squat from Neck

This stunt is performed in the same manner as the straddle from neck, except the legs remain together and the knees and waist bend until the feet clear the horse.

Safety: Same as for the stand on croup and straddle from neck.

PHYSICAL PRINCIPLES INVOLVED IN VAULTING

A few of the scientific principles involved in executing side-horse and long-horse vaults are listed as follows:

1. A body may be put into motion by the transfer of momentum from a body part to the whole.

Example: In performing the neckspring vault on the side horse, the forward extension of the legs causes the head and shoulders to rise to an upright position.

2. For every force there is always an equal and opposite counterforce.

Example: As the gymnast leaves the beatboard, his legs must be extended and his body stretched so as to produce the maximum reaction upward from the board.

3. A body will turn slower when the length of the radius of rotation about the center of gravity is increased.

> **Example:** In performing the front-handspring vault over the side horse, the turn is slower when the arms and legs are extended. Since the extension of the arms and legs is considered correct, there must be a greater effort on takeoff to compensate for the slower rotation.

4. The height to which the vaulter rises above the horse depends upon the amount the beatboard is depressed, the angle of takeoff (lean), and the push of the hands (in some instances) on the horse.

> **Example:** The effects of each of the named factors can be seen in the execution of a straddle vault over the side horse.

5. In vaulting stunts, the center of gravity should fall as nearly as possible over the point of support.

> **Example:** In performing the straddle vault over the long horse, the center of gravity moves in the direction of the vault and the straddle-off is executed at the peak of the lift above the horse.

6. The static balance of a body is indirectly proportional to the distance of the center of gravity of that body above its base.

> **Example:** In making a steady landing from a long-horse vault, it is important to lower the center of gravity by bending the knees upon contact with the mat. This also aids in absorbing the shock of the dismount (by spending the force of the landing over a distance).

7. In vaulting stunts where horizontal distance is needed, maximum speed should be attained at the moment of takeoff.

Example: In performing vaults over the long horse, it is important not to slow down the run prior to takeoff. Failure to observe this principle causes many beginners to land on the horse rather than on the mats at the far end.

9

Parallel-bars Stunts

In the learning of parallel-bars stunts, the bars should be raised or lowered as the nature of the stunt and the needs of the individual dictate. The first sixteen of the following stunts may be learned with the bars set at a low level.

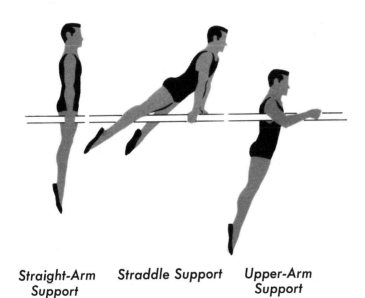

Straight-Arm Support   **Straddle Support**   **Upper-Arm Support**

Handwalk on Bars

From a standing position between the bars, jump to a straight-arm support and handwalk the length of the bars, keeping the legs together and the arms straight. Movement down the bars is achieved by leaning on one arm and stepping forward with the opposite hand. Take small steps with the hand and do not rush. This stunt emphasizes the importance of proper position and extension in movement.

Swing-Hop and Catch

From a straight-arm support between the bars, swing the legs forward causing the body to pike; at the same time hop forward by moving both hands simultaneously. As the hands regrasp, the legs swing downward and backward. Hop each time the legs swing forward. Do not bend the arms as the hop or catch is made.

Swing from a Straight-Arm Support

From a straight-arm support between the bars, lift the legs forward and extend the body into an arched position, allowing the legs to drive downward and backward. Lean slightly forward as the legs go to the rear and lean slightly backward as they move toward the front again. Do not let the elbows bend during the swing and remember that a good swing makes parallel-bar work easy.

Cross-Straddle Seat-Travel

From a straight-arm support between the bars, swing the legs forward causing them to split and rest on top of the bars. Lean the body forward, release the hands from behind, and regrasp the bars in front of the legs. Continue to lean forward, keeping the arms and legs straight, and lift the legs off of the bars, allowing them to swing forward again to the straddle-seat position. These movements may be repeated until the length of the bars has been traveled.

Front Dismount

From a straight-arm support between the bars, swing the legs forward, allowing them to drive downward and backward until they are well above the bars. As the legs reach their peak at the backswing, push with the right hand, causing the body to shift over the left bar. As the body begins its drop toward the mat, the right hand grasps in front of the left hand while the left hand is released and extended to the side. The right hand remains on the bar to steady the performer as he lands. This stunt may be executed to the left or right.

Safety: A mat may be draped over the left bar behind the left hand. Also, a spotter may grasp the left wrist of the performer and pull outward as the left hand is released.

Rear Dismount

Swinging from a straight-arm support, allow the legs to swing forward and reach a height slightly above the bars. Push with the left hand, causing the body weight to lean on the right hand. As the body is shifted over the right bar, the left hand releases the left bar and regrasps in front of the right hand on the right bar. The right hand is then released and extended to the side. The left hand remains on the near bar to steady the performer as he lands. This stunt may be performed to the left or right.

Safety: A mat may be draped over the right bar in front of the right hand. Also, a spotter may grasp the right wrist and pull outward as the right hand is released.

Front Dismount One-Half Turn

Swinging from a straight-arm support between the bars, allow the legs to reach a height well above the bars on the backswing. Push hard as you release the right hand, causing the body to shift over the left bar. The left hand is released momentarily as the thumb of the left hand is switched from inside the left bar to outside the left bar. As the left hand shifts to its new position, the body turns outward from the near bar, making a half-turn. The left hand remains on the left bar to steady the performer as he lands. This stunt may be performed to the left or right.

Safety: Drape a mat over the left bar behind the left hand so that the body makes its turn over the covered bar.

Rear Dismount One-Half Turn Inward

Swinging from a straight-arm support between the bars, allow the legs to swing forward slightly higher than the bars. Push hard as you release both hands, causing the body to shift over the right bar. As the body clears the bar, make a half-turn inward (toward the bar) and grasp the bar with the right hand to steady the landing.

The left hand is extended to the side for balance. This stunt may be executed to the left or right.

Single-Leg Cut and Catch Mount

From a stand outside of the bars and facing the ends of the bars, grasp each bar and jump toward a straight-arm support. Before reaching the straight-arm support, split the legs and allow the right leg to pass over the right bar and under the right hand. Regrasp with the right hand and let the right leg drop between the bars while a straight-arm support is maintained. Be sure and lean on the left hand as the right hand is released and do not allow either arm to bend during the stunt. Students should learn the single-leg cut and catch using either leg.

Flank Cut and Catch Mount

From a stand outside of the bars and facing the ends of the bars, grasp each bar and jump toward a straight-arm support. Before reaching the straight-arm support position, lean on the left hand and allow both legs to swing over the right bar and under the right hand. Regrasp with the right hand and let the legs drop between the bars while a straight-arm support is maintained. Students should learn to flank to each side and remember that the arms should be kept straight throughout the sunt.

Safety: Same as for the single-leg cut and catch dismount.

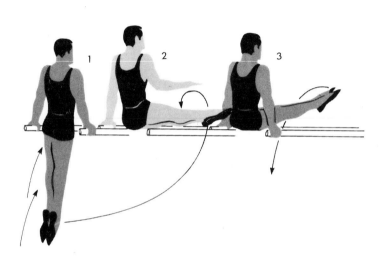

Straddle Cut and Catch Mount

From a stand outside of the bars and facing the ends of the bars, grasp each bar and jump toward a straight-arm support. Before reaching the straight-arm support position, push hard with both hands as the release is made and allow the legs to separate with each leg passing over the bar and under the corresponding hand. Regrasp with both hands and let the legs rejoin and drop between the bars as a straight-arm support is maintained.

Safety: Same as for the single-leg cut and catch dismount.

Straddle Dismount

Swinging from a straight-arm support between the ends of the bars and facing outward, allow the legs to swing backward until they reach a peak well above the bars. Allow the shoulders to lean slightly forward and push with the hands as the legs separate and pass over the bars and under the hands. The legs rejoin as the performer lands on his feet on the mat below.

Safety: Standing outside and slightly forward of the end of the right bar, the spotter grasps the performer's right wrist with the left hand. As the performer releases his hands from the bars, the spotter steps away from the bars, assisting the performer in flight. The right hand of the spotter may be placed on the performer's chest if difficulty occurs on the landing.

Flank Mount with Mixed Grip

From a stand outside of the bars facing the center of the near bar, place the right hand on the bar using a reverse grasp and the left hand on the same bar using a regular grasp. Jump, causing the hips and legs to rise higher than the bar, and at the same time lean the shoulders directly over the hands. The arms should be extending as the hips rise. Release with the left hand and while leaning on the right hand, turn the head and shoulders to the right, causing the body to turn and drop between the bars. As the body begins its turn over the near bar, regrasp the far bar with the left hand and swing between the bars. This stunt may be executed to the left or right.

Safety: Drape a mat over the near bar next to the left hand so that the body can turn over a covered bar.

Forward Roll in Straddle Position

From a straddle-seat position, grasp the bars in front of the legs and lean forward until the shoulders or upper arms contact the bars. With the elbows turned down to the outside, raise the hips until they lean slightly over the shoulders. Keeping the body in a pike position, release the grasp of both hands, crossing them on the lower part of the back to allow the roll to continue onto the arms until the performer reaches the straddle-seat position again. As the release is made with the hands, the performer must keep the elbows turned down to the outside, maintaining a straddle position with the legs.

Safety: Standing on the outside of the bars, the spotter places his right hand under the near bar with the palm of the hand against the performer's back. The spotter's left hand assists the performer in keeping the elbows turned downward.

Shoulder Stand

From a straddle-seat position, grasp the bars in front of the legs and lean forward until the shoulders or upper arms contact the bars. Keeping the elbows turned down to the outside, raise the hips until they attain a vertical position overhead. Holding the head up, extend the legs until they are directly overhead and together. At this point, assume a slight arch and point the toes. To get out of the shoulder stand safely, pike at the waist, separate the legs and lower to the starting position, or roll forward performing the straddle roll as described in the forward roll.

Safety: Same as for the forward roll.

Single-Leg Cut One-Half Turn

From a straight-arm support, swing the legs forward, crossing the right leg over the left bar while leaning on the left arm, and releasing the right hand from the right bar. At this point, the right hand grasps the left bar so that the right leg is between the left and right hands. The weight is now shifted to the right hand, and the right leg cuts under the left hand and back in between the bars as the left hand releases and then regrasps the opposite bar. The performer is now back in a straight-arm support, but facing in the opposite direction. Throughout the stunt, the left leg remains between the bars. This stunt may be executed to the left or right.

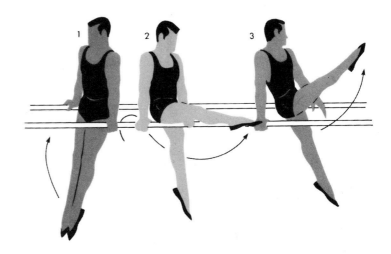

Back Uprise

From an upper-arm support, swing the legs forward and upward until the knees are piked approximately above the face. At this point, extend the legs forward and downward while maintaining a slight pike in the hips. At the bottom of the swing, drive the heels and hips backward into a forceful arch and pull hard with the hands, causing the feet to rise above the bars in the rear. As the shoulders move forward, the arms are extended into a straight-arm support position. During the swing downward and backward, do not allow the shoulders to sag between the bars since this slows down the swing.

Hip-Kip Straddle

From an upper-arm support, swing the legs forward and upward until the knees are piked approximately above the face. At this point, extend the legs forward and at the same time pull forcefully with the hands so that the head and shoulders rise as the legs separate and lower onto the bars. The stunt is completed with the performer in a straddle position on the bars with straight arms.

Safety: The spotter moves one hand under and between the bars placing it on the performer's buttocks while moving the other hand over the near bar and placing it behind the performer's neck. From this position he may assist the performer in the execution of the stunt.

Hip-Kip-Up

This stunt is performed in the same manner as the hip-kip straddle except that the legs remain together throughout the execution. This allows the performer to complete the stunt in a straight-arm support position.

Safety: Same as for the hip-kip straddle.

Drop Kip

With the hands on the ends of the bars, fingers curling over the bars toward the outside, jump slightly upward and pull with the arms (don't bend the elbows) so that the head and shoulders lean to the rear as the legs swing forward into a pike position with the knees over the face. Allow the body to swing forward while keeping the elbows straight. As the body swings backward, extend the legs upward and forward while pulling with the arms. The performer's head and shoulders should rise as the legs lower so that the stunt is completed in a straight-arm support. This stunt may also be performed in the middle of the bars by dropping back into a pike position from a straight-arm support above the bars.

Safety: By placing one hand on the buttocks and one hand on the back of the neck, the spotter may assist the performer in the execution of the stunt.

Routine

Combine five or six stunts into a

routine which is in some way different from the routines of other members in the class.

PHYSICAL PRINCIPLES INVOLVED IN WORK ON THE PARALLEL BARS

A few of the scientific principles involved in executing parallel bar sunts are listed as follows:

1. In mounting stunts which involve swinging or rotary movement, the center of gravity should be brought as close to the center of support or rotation as possible at the crucial moment.

Example: In performing the drop kip, the center of gravity must stay as close as possible to the center of rotation (the hands). Failure to comply with this principle creates a moment of force in which the center of gravity cannot be shifted over the hands as the head and shoulders rise.

2. The center of gravity must be kept over the point of support in swinging on the parallel bars.

Example: In swinging from a straight-arm support, the shoulders should lean slightly to the rear as the feet swing forward and vice versa as the feet swing to the rear.

3. In swinging stunts, centrifugal force is least near the peak of the swing.

Example: In executing a straddle dismount from the parallel bars, the legs should reach a peak well above the bars before the cut between the hands and the bars is made.

4. A body may be put into motion by the transfer of momentum from a body part to the whole.

Example: In performing the hip-kip-up, the legs extend forward, causing the body to rise above the bars.

5. In swinging on the parallel bars, decreasing the radius of rotation (distance between the center of gravity and center of support) on the swing upward will accelerate the movement while increasing the radius on the downswing increases the linear velocity of the center of gravity at the bottom of the swing.

> **Example:** This may be accomplished by swinging on the parallel bars from a straight-arm support by flexing the hips on the upswing, and by extending the hips at the beginning of the downswing.

6. Twisting movements which are started while the body is on a rotating support will be in the direction of the movement of those parts of the body which are used to initiate it.

> **Example:** In executing the single-leg cut half-turn to the left, the rotating support is initially the left arm, and the twist to the left is caused by the turning of the head, shoulders, and hips to the left.

7. In swinging stunts, the act of pulling toward the center of support along the line of the radius when the center of gravity is under the point of support gives an added boost, causing the center of gravity to rise.

> **Example:** In executing the back uprise on the parallel bars, pulling when the center of gravity is directly below the point of support (upper arms) facilitates performance.

8. The static balance of a body is directly proportional to the area of the base on which the body is supported.

> **Example:** In holding a shoulder stand on the parallel bars, a wider base is created by turning the elbows out to the side so that the hands and shoulders form four points of support.

10

Horizontal-bar
Stunts

The following stunts are explained in a simple to complex order, but may be considered as somewhat flexible. Many of the stunts may be performed with the bar low or high. Therefore, the bar should be adjusted in accordance with the nature of the stunt and the desires of the students. If the bar is lowered, it should be placed at about 4½ to 5 feet, and if raised, not above 8 feet.

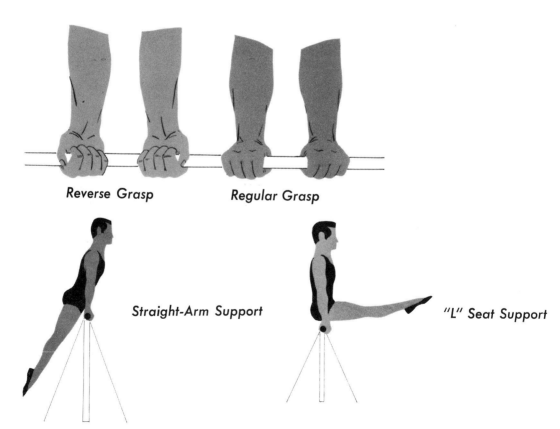

Reverse Grasp   Regular Grasp

Straight-Arm Support   "L" Seat Support

German Hang

Grasp the bar with a regular grip and while bending at the knees and waist, pull the legs upward between the arms and under the bar. Continue to extend the feet to the rear and downward until steady resistance is met in the shoulders. At the completion of the stunt, return to the starting position.

Safety: The performer should maintain a piked position with the knees close to the chest as he lowers downward.

German Hang—One Full Turn

This stunt is executed in the same manner as the German hang, except upon meeting a steady resistance in the shoulders, turn loose with the left hand and hang on with the right hand until a full turn has been completed. At the completion of the turn, re-grasp with the left hand. This stunt may be performed to the left or right.

Safety: Avoid a jerk in the right shoulder by making sure that both shoulders are fully extended before the release. A spotter may stand behind the performer grasping the hips and assisting the performer through the full turn.

Back Pullover

Using a regular grasp, pull the head and chest upward toward the bar with a chinning (flexing or pulling) action of the arms. Continue to pull with the arms while piking at the waist and raising the legs and hips upward over the top of the bar. As the upper-abdominal region contacts the bar, the feet lower downward to the rear, causing the head and shoulders to rise above the bar, finishing in a straight-arm support.

Safety: Standing under the bar and to the side of the performer, the spotter assists by pressing upward on the performer's shoulder as the hips and legs pass over the bar. The performer should avoid placing the lower-abdominal region against the bar since this will not allow enough body weight to the rear to cause the head and shoulders to rise smoothly.

Knee-Kip-Up

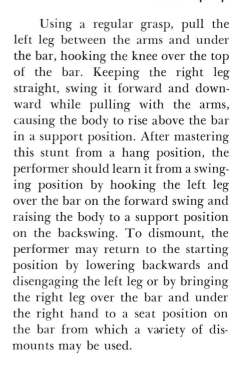

Using a regular grasp, pull the left leg between the arms and under the bar, hooking the knee over the top of the bar. Keeping the right leg straight, swing it forward and downward while pulling with the arms, causing the body to rise above the bar in a support position. After mastering this stunt from a hang position, the performer should learn it from a swinging position by hooking the left leg over the bar on the forward swing and raising the body to a support position on the backswing. To dismount, the performer may return to the starting position by lowering backwards and disengaging the left leg or by bringing the right leg over the bar and under the right hand to a seat position on the bar from which a variety of dismounts may be used.

Safety: Standing to the side of the performer and slightly forward, the spotter assists the performer should he fail to stop in a support on top of the bar.

ONE LINE LONG

Underswing Dismount

From a straight-arm support above the bar with a regular grasp, drop the shoulders backward and at the same time pike at the waist and pull with the arms, causing the feet to shoot upward and outward. At the completion of the pull, arch the back and push with the hands as you release the bar. The performer should land in a standing position.

Safety: Standing to the side and slightly forward of the bar, the spotter assists the performer in getting the hips high and in steadying the performer on the landing.

Pick-Up Swing and Simple-Back Dismount

Using a regular grasp, pull the body up toward the bar and at the same time pike at the waist, causing the feet to rise higher than the bar. When the feet attain this height, push with the arms, extending the legs upward and outward while arching the back. This enables the performer to obtain a good swing. As the body swings to the rear, pull with the arms and pike at the waist, letting the hips ride high. As the hips reach their peak, push downward on the bar, release, and straighten the body position for the landing.

Safety: Standing under the bar and to the side of the performer, the spotter should assist the performer in getting his hips up on the forward swing and maintain close hand contact with the performer until the downward push with the hands has been executed, in preparation for the dismount.

Kip-Up

Grasping the bar with a regular grip, swing forward and backward. As the body swings forward again, arch the back and at the peak of the forward swing quickly pike at the hips, bringing the insteps of the feet close to the bar. Maintain this piked position with the insteps near the bar until the hips swing backward between the uprights; extend the legs upward and outward as you pull and press the body above the bar with straight arms. The bar should remain close to the legs as they extend upward and outward. As the legs start downward, the hips should contact the bar smoothly. This stunt may also be learned with a reverse grip.

Safety: Standing under the bar and on the right side of the performer, the spotter may give assistance by placing the left hand on the performer's buttocks and the right hand on the back of the performer's right thigh. As the performer kicks and pulls, the spotter pushes and assists him to a straight-arm support.

Drop Kip

From a straight-arm support above the bar, the performer lowers backwards, piking at the waist and bringing the insteps of the feet close to the bar. Maintain this piked position with the insteps near the bar until the hips swing backward between the uprights. When the hips have passed the vertical uprights, kick the legs upward and outward and press the body above the bar in the same manner as demonstrated in the previous stunt.

Safety: Same as for the kip-up.

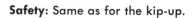

Back-Hip Circle

From a straight-arm support above the bar, lean slightly forward and push the hips backward away from the bar while arching the back. As the hips swing forward and contact the bar, pike and lower the shoulders backwards rotating the body around the bar by pulling inward and keeping the hips against the bar.

Safety: Standing under the bar (lowered for spotting purposes) and to the right side of the performer, the spotter grasps the performer's right wrist from the back side of the bar with the hand turned so that the thumb is on the under side of the wrist and the fingers are on the top side of the wrist. As the performer rotates around the bar, the spotter's right hand assists the performer in keeping close to the bar.

Forward-Hip Circle

From a straight-arm support above the bar with a regular grasp, slightly pike at the hips, causing the bar to rest against the upper thighs. Roll the head and shoulders forward (the neck should be extended so that the head is well forward at the start) as fast as possible while slipping the bar from the upper thighs to the abdominal region as the body rotates around the bar. Remember to keep the bar against the body throughout the stunt and slip the grasp, prior to the body leaning forward, into a support at the completion of the stunt.

Safety: As the performer rotates to the inverted position, the spotter may assist by pushing against the underside of the thigh, thus assisting the performer back to a support over the bar.

Circus Kip

From a hang below the bar with a regular grasp, develop a very slight swing, force the hips upward on the front swing, causing the back to arch. As the hips drop downward on the backswing, pike and forcefully pull with the arms, causing the body to snap upward into a straight-arm support above the bar. In the final phase, the pull of the arms transfers to a push. There should be no hesitation between the two.

Safety: Same as for the kip-up.

Back Up-Rise

From a hang below the bar using a regular grasp, cast the body upward and outward, developing a forceful swing to the rear. As the body gets directly under the bar, pull and continue the swing rearward while piking slightly at the hips. Prior to contacting the bar with the hips, the chest should be extended outward and the back arched. If the beginner is leery of contacting the bar with the hips, he may drop the shoulders as he nears the bar and perform a back-hip circle.

Safety: Standing to the side of the performer and slightly to the rear, the spotter may push on the performer's near leg, just above the knee, causing the hips to rise higher on the backswing.

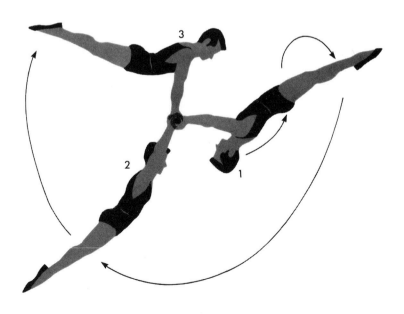

Back Kip-Up

From a hang below the bar using a regular grasp, cast the body upward, outward, downward, and to the rear. As the body swings forward, ride the hips high and quickly pike at the hips, keeping the legs straight or bending at the knees, and bring the feet under the bar and between the arms. Maintain a tight pike, keeping the lower part of the legs close to the bar on the swing to the rear. As the swing forward begins, keep the legs and seat close to the bar by maintaining a steady pull while arching the back and lifting the head up. As the head, shoulders, and hips rise above the bar, slip the seat over the bar to a sitting position.

Safety: Standing to the side of the performer and directly under the bar, the spotter assists the performer by pushing under the hips as he arches the back and looks up.

Pike-Seat Rise

From a hang below the bar using a reverse grasp, cast the body upward, outward, downward, and to the rear. As the body swings forward, ride the hips high and pike quickly, bringing the feet under the bar and between arms. Maintain a tight pike as the body swings to the rear and pull with the arms, continuing the rearward swing until the body is over the bar in a seat position. Be sure and force the head and shoulders forward as the pull begins on the rearward swing and do not allow the back to arch.

Safety: Standing to the side of the spotter and directly under the bar, the spotter assists the performer by pushing under the hips as he begins his pike rise toward the top of the bar.

Back-Leanover Dismount

From a sitting position on top of the bar, drop the head and shoulders backward while arching the back and releasing the hands. Force the feet to remain on the forward side of the bar until they are whipped over by the tension of the arched back. The performer should land in a standing position below the bar.

Safety: Use two spotters if possible. One spotter insures that the feet remain on the forward side of the bar until the back is completely arched. The other spotter stands to the side of the performer and slightly to the rear of the bar. He supports the performer's near shoulder as he leans backward and releases the bar.

Routine

Combine five or six stunts into a routine which is in some way different from the routines of other members of the class.

PHYSICAL PRINCIPLES INVOLVED IN HORIZONTAL-BAR WORK

A few of the scientific principles involved in executing horizontal bar stunts are listed as follows:

1. The total effective force may be the summation of the forces of each body part if applied in one direction and in the proper succession.

    Example: In performing stunts such as the circus kip which necessitate pulling the body up and then pushing it further upward, there should be no hesitation between the pull-up and the push.

2. In mounting stunts which involve swinging or rotary motion, the center of gravity should be brought as close to the center of support or rotation as possible at the crucial moment.

> **Example:** In executing the back pull-over on the horizontal bar, the center of gravity is held against the bar and above it as the body rotates until it establishes its equilibrium.

3. In swinging on the horizontal bar, decreasing the radius of rotation (distance between the center of gravity and the center of support) on the swing upward will accelerate the movement while increasing the radius on the downswing increases the linear velocity of the center of gravity at the bottom of the swing.

> **Example:** This may be accomplished by swinging on the horizontal bar from a hang, flexing the hips and arms at the start of the upswing, and extending the hips and arms at the beginning of the downswing.

4. In swinging stunts, the act of pulling toward the center of support along the line of the radius when the center of gravity is under the point of support gives an added boost, causing the center of gravity to rise.

> **Example:** In executing the back up-rise on the bar, pulling when the center of gravity is directly below the point of support facilitates the performance.

5. For every force there is an equal and opposite counterforce.

> **Example:** In executing the back-lean-over dismount, the force of the body dropping back to a horizontal position and the subsequent extension of the hips produces a counterforce against the bar which enables the performer to whip the legs around in time to land on the feet.

6. A body may be put into motion by the transfer of momentum from a body part to the whole.

> **Example:** In executing the knee-kip-up on the bar, swinging the free leg forward and downward causes the head and shoulders to rise.

11

Still-rings Stunts

In learning the following stunts, adjust the rings high or low in accordance with the nature of the stunt and the expressed desires of the students. Due to the weakness of the arms and shoulders of most beginners, it is recommended that the following safety techniques be observed closely.

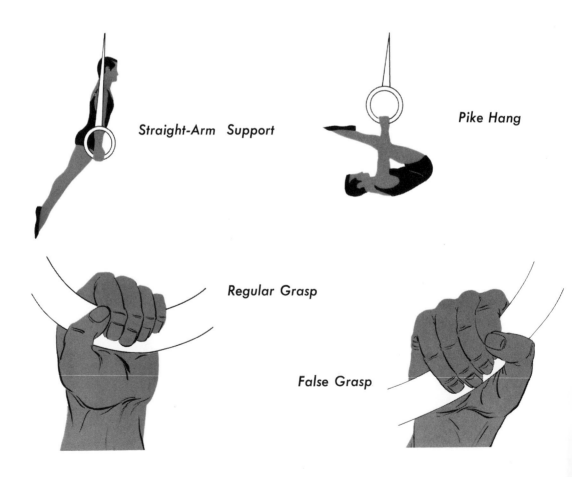

Straight-Arm Support

Pike Hang

Regular Grasp

False Grasp

German Hang

Grasp the rings and pike at the waist, bringing the feet upward and over the head. Continue moving the feet from an over-the-head position downward until steady resistance is met in the shoulders. Keep the legs straight and toes pointed from the start. At the completion of the stunt, return to the starting position.

Safety: The spotter should assist the performer in getting his hips up and in maintaining a piked position. When strength and confidence improves, the spotter will not be needed.

Bird's Nest

Grasp the rings and pike at the waist, bringing the feet upward and between the rings. Engage the rings with the feet and arch the body below the rings until a steady resistance is met in the back. At the completion of the stunt, return to the starting position by ducking the head and bending at the hips.

Safety: A spotter should be on the alert and ready to assist should a weak student disengage his feet while in the arched position. In such a case, the spotter should grasp the performer's near arm just above the elbow and place the other hand on the chest.

Inverted Hang

Grasp the rings and pike at the waist, bringing the feet upward between the straps. As the feet get between the straps, extend the legs and hips until they are directly overhead. This position should be maintained with the neck extended, body slightly arched, legs straight and together, with the toes pointed. Do not allow the elbows to bend while maintaining this balance. After holding for a few seconds, return to the starting position.

Safety: The beginner may rest his legs against the straps while maintaining the inverted position for the first few trials. A spotter may assist the performer in assuming the correct position by placing one hand on the performer's chest and one hand on the back.

Single-Leg Cut Dismount

Grasp the rings and pike at the waist, bringing the feet upward between and beyond the rings until the knees are directly over the face. Swing forward separating the legs, causing the left leg to return between the rings and the right leg to cut between the right ring and the right hand as the grasp is released with both hands. Prior to the release, roll the head and shoulders forward with a definite force. The performer lands on his feet with the arms extended to the sides for balance. This stunt may be executed to either side.

Safety: The spotter stands behind the performer placing the left hand on the back of the performer's neck and assists by pressing upward as the performer releases his grasp. The right hand of the spotter grasps the performer's waist to prevent an overthrow on the landing.

Single-Leg Straddle Dismount

Grasp the rings and swing the legs forward and then backward. As the legs swing forward again, pull with the arms and pike at the waist, causing the feet to rise well above the rings. Separate the legs, allowing the right leg to go between the straps and the left leg to pass between the left hand and the left ring as both rings are released. The head should be turned backward as the release is made to give the performer more momentum. As the performer lands on his feet, the arms should be extended to the sides for balance.

Safety: Standing on the right side of the performer, the spotter places his right hand on the performer's chest as the performer turns upside down and grasps the performer's upper arm with the left hand to prevent overturning.

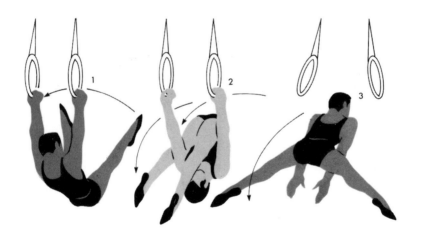

Double-Leg Cut Dismount

Grasp the rings and pike at the waist, bringing the feet upward between and beyond the rings until the knees are directly over the face. Swing forward separating the legs, causing the right leg to cut between the right ring and right hand and the left leg to cut between the left ring and left hand as the grasp is released with both hands. Prior to the release, the head and shoulders must roll forward with a definite force.

Safety: Same as for the single-leg cut dismount.

Double-Leg Straddle Dismount

This stunt is performed in the same manner as single-leg straddle dismount, except that as the legs separate the rings are pulled close together and both legs pass between the rings and the hands as the hands release. Remember to pull hard with the arms and turn the head backward to get enough momentum to land on the feet.

Safety: Same as for the single-leg straddle dismount.

Single-Leg Kip-Up

Grasp the rings and pike at the waist, bringing the feet upward between and beyond the rings until the knees are directly over the face. Forcefully roll the head and shoulders forward, causing the legs to separate and swing forward. The right leg passes between the rings driving outward and downward as the left leg hooks over the left wrist next to the left ring. The performer pulls with the arms and presses with the left leg as the body moves above the rings. After maintaining this position for a few seconds, return to the starting position. The pressing action of the leg may be executed to either side.

Safety: Standing on the right side, the spotter places the right hand on the performer's right knee as the right leg drives downward and pushes with the left hand under the buttocks.

Dislocate

Grasp the rings and pike at the waist, bringing the feet upward between and beyond the rings until the knees are directly over the face. Extend the legs backward while arching the back and keeping the arms straight.

As the legs extend to the rear, spread the arms and shoulders to avoid a jerk at the bottom of the swing.

Safety: If possible, for the first few times, use two spotters on this stunt. One spotter lifts on the chest while the other spotter lifts on the feet until the shoulders have dislocated.

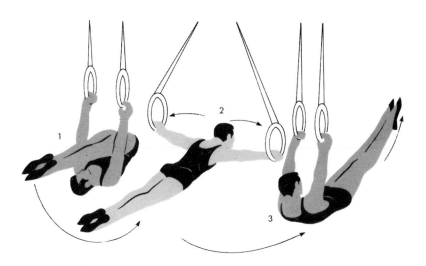

Inlocate

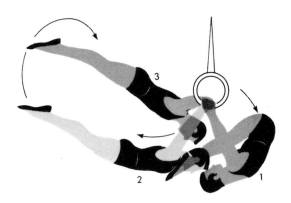

Grasp the rings, swinging the legs forward and then backward. As the legs reach their peak on the backswing, turn the rings inward while ducking the head forward and piking at the waist. The stunt is completed in a pike hang below the rings with the knees directly above the face. The first few tries may be made while standing on an object two or three feet high. The performer jumps, pushing his hips upward into the pike position while ducking the head and turning the rings inward.

Safety: As the performer's legs swing backward, the spotter, while standing on the right side, places his right hand on the performer's right hip and the left hand slightly above the perform-er's right knee. In this position, the spotter assists the performer in reaching his peak swing prior to the in-locate action of the shoulders.

Muscle-Up

Grasp the rings and while pulling the shoulders upward and bending at the elbows, cause the grip of each hand to shift from the outside of the rings to the inside. Do not release the rings with the thumbs, but keep them around the rings. This change of the grip should place the inside of each wrist against the inside of the corresponding ring. This is known as a "false grip." Using the false grip, the performer executes the muscle-up by pulling the head and shoulders upward and at the same time piking at the waist. As the shoulders lean forward over the hands, the arms cease to pull and begin on the push or extension to a straight-arm support above the rings. As the change is made from the pull to the push position, do not let the arms get wider than shoulder width apart.

Safety: Standing on the right side of the rings, the spotter places the right hand slightly above the right knee of the performer with the thumb on the underside. The left hand is placed on the underside of the right buttocks. As the performer pulls, the spotter pushes, assisting the performer in his first few efforts to get above the rings.

Double-Leg Kip-Up

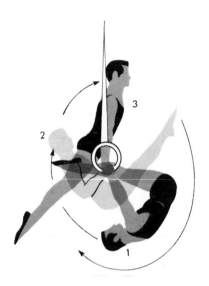

Grasping the rings, using a false or regular grip, pull the legs upward until the knees are directly over the face. Push the legs upward and forward between the rings and at the same time pull with the arms. As the legs begin to drop downward, the head and shoulders rise above the rings in a straight-arm support.

Safety: Standing on the right side, the spotter places the left hand between the performer's shoulders and the right hand on the right buttocks. From this position, the spotter assists the performer to the straight-arm-support position.

"L" Position

From a straight-arm support above the rings, the performer pikes at the waist until the legs are parallel to the floor. In this position, the head is held erect, chest out, legs straight and together, toes pointed, and the rings are turned slightly outward away from the hips.

Safety: Learn to hold the "L" on the parallel bars before attempting it in the rings. Also, when first learning to perform on the rings, hold the rings close to the hips.

Single-Leg Front Lever

From an inverted hang below the rings, bend the right knee, placing the side of the right foot against the side of the left knee and lower the body until the back side of the body is parallel to the mat below. In this position hold the head back, chest up, back straight or slightly arched, and the left leg straight with the toes pointed. The position should be held approximately three seconds with the elbows straight.

Safety: Standing to the side of the performer, the spotter places one hand under the performer's hips and the other hand under the left knee, giving assistance to the performer until he develops the necessary strength to perform the stunt without help.

Beginner's Cross

Standing on a partner's shoulders, slip each hand between the canvas straps and grasp the lower part of the ring. Direct the partner to move and then lower into the cross position with the arms extending horizontally to the sides. The straps should support the forearms as the arms extend outward. After holding several seconds, direct the partner to again move under the rings for support.

Shoulder Stand

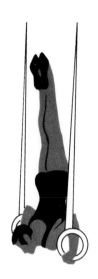

From a straight-arm support above the rings in the "L" position, bend at the elbows, allowing the shoulders to lower between the rings and the hips to rise between the straps. Keeping the head up, extend the legs overhead while turning the rings slightly outward, thus forcing the bent elbows next to the sides of the body. Keep the back slightly arched, toes pointed, and legs straight.

Safety: In learning the shoulder stand, separate the legs as the hips rise between the straps so that the back of the legs rest against the straps. With consistent practice, the performer should come to depend less and less on the use of the straps. Should the performer fall forward out of the rings, the spotter may slow the fall by pressing against the small of the performer's back.

Routine

Combine five or six stunts into a routine which is in some way different from the routines of other members of the class.

PHYSICAL PRINCIPLES INVOLVED IN STILL-RINGS WORK

A few of the scientific principles involved in executing still-rings stunts are listed as follows:

1. In swinging on the still rings, decreasing the radius of rotation on the swing upward will accelerate the movement while increasing the radius on the down-swing increases the linear velocity of the center of gravity at the bottom of the swing.

Example: This may be accomplished by swinging on the still rings from a hang, flexing the hips and elbows at the start of the upswing, and extending the hips and arms at the beginning of the downswing.

2. The total effective force may be the summation of the forces of each member of each body part if applied in one direction and in proper succession.

> **Example:** In performing stunts such as the muscle-up which necessitate pulling the body up and then pushing it further upward, there should be no hesitation between the pull-up and the push.

3. In swinging stunts, the act of pulling toward the center of support along the line of the radius when the center of gravity is directly under the point of support gives an added boost causing the center of gravity to rise.

> **Example:** In swinging for a straddle dismount, a hard pull at the bottom of the swing facilitates the execution of the stunt.

4. A body may be put into motion by the transfer of momentum from a body part to the whole.

> **Example:** In executing a double-leg kip-up in the rings, extending the legs upward and outward causes the head and shoulders to rise.

5. To maintain static balance, the center of gravity of an object must fall within its base.

> **Example:** In holding a shoulderstand in the rings, the performer's center of gravity is maintained within its base by turning the rings to the outside when the feet lean too far forward, and by turning the rings inward when the feet lean too far to the rear.

6. In swinging stunts, centrifugal force is least near the peak of the swing.

> **Example:** In executing a straddle dismount from the rings, the legs should reach a peak well above the rings before they cut between the hands and the rings.

12

Rebound-tumbling Stunts

The following rebound-tumbling or trampoline stunts are arranged in a simple to complex order, however there is room for flexibility of arrangement. It should be emphasized that students work quickly on trampoline stunts, taking about three or four tries at each turn on the apparatus with as few extra bounces as possible. Otherwise, several students may monopolize the trampoline for the major portion of the period.

Mount

There are two methods which the performer may use to properly mount onto the trampoline. He may crawl on by using the hands and legs or he may place the hands on the frame, jump the hips upward while ducking the head, and execute a forward roll into the middle.

Dismount

There are many ways to get off of a trampoline; however, there is only one proper way for beginners. The beginner should reach forward and place the right hand and the left foot on the frame. Keeping the weight on the right arm, he should hop the right foot between the left foot and right arm and drop to the floor, bending at the knees on the landing.

Spotting Technique

There should be one spotter for each of the four sides of the trampoline. If the performer is falling at a low angle toward the frame, the spotter should lean forward and push the performer back so that he does not contact it. If the performer is bounding from the trampoline at a high angle and it appears that he will miss the frame, the spotter should grasp the performer's arm or shoulder and step backward, allowing him to land his feet on the floor.

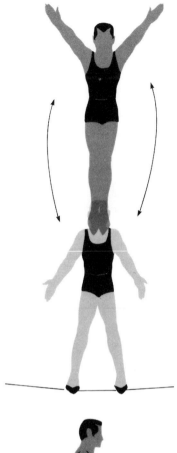

Proper-Bounce Technique

The performer should learn to bounce by keeping the feet a step apart as he lands on the canvas and placing the feet together while in the air. The arms should be raised upward on the ascent and lowered to the sides on the descent. The body should sustain an upright position with the eyes maintaining contact with the mat.

Tuck Bounce

Bounce upward and draw the knees up to the chest by bending at the knees and waist. Grasp the shins with the hands and quickly release and straighten out for the descent.

Pike Bounce

Bounce upward and lift the legs so that they are straight and parallel to the canvas. Touch the shins with the hands and quickly straighten out for the descent. Be sure to lift the legs enough so that the upper body does not have to lean too far forward to touch the shins. The body should be bent only at the waist.

Straddle Bounce

This stunt is executed in the same manner as the pike bounce, except the legs should split as wide as possible while in the pike position.

Seat Drop

Drop straight down to the canvas in a sitting position, so that the back of the heels and the seat contact the canvas at the same time. The head and shoulders should maintain an upright position and the hands should contact the mat on each side of the seat with the fingers pointing toward the feet. Push with the hands and return to the feet. Avoid jumping forward into a seat drop.

Knee Drop

Keeping the body in an upright position, bend the knees at the peak of a bounce and drop to the canvas, landing on the knees, shins, and insteps. Avoid arching the back on this stunt since it could cause a strained back. To regain the feet, bounce from the canvas by raising the arms and lifting the knees and toes off the mat together. A tendency to get the knees up early and ride back on the toes frequently causes the performer to bounce backwards out of control.

Hands and Knee Drop

From a low bounce, tilt the upper body slightly forward and bend at the knees. Don't jump forward, but drop to the canvas so that the knees and hands contact the canvas together. The arms should be kept straight and the hands should contact the canvas directly under each shoulder. To regain the feet, push with the hands, driving the head and shoulders upward while bringing the feet back in line under the body.

Knee Drop—Front Drop

From a low bounce, perform the knee drop in the center of the canvas. As the performer rebounds upward from the canvas, he should push the hips upward and backward, assuming a piked position. As the performer nears the canvas, he should stretch out of the piked position and land the beltline in the same spot that the knees had previously left from. In the landing position, the performer should be in a straight-prone position with the arms forward and elbows bent to the sides. The neck should be held rigid so that the performer's chin will not contact the canvas. The hands, forearms, abdomen, thighs, knees, and insteps should contact the mat simultaneously. Make the beltline land where the feet left from, thus avoiding a dive forward. To regain the feet, push with the hands and forearms, driving the head and chest upward and bringing the feet under the body.

Front Drop

This stunt is executed in the same manner as the knee drop–front drop, except that it is performed from the feet rather than the knees. Remember to avoid diving forward on this stunt.

Back Drop

From a stand in the middle of the canvas, lift one leg upward, lean backward, and kick the other leg upward. As you drop to the canvas, pike at the waist with the eyes fixed on the knees. The hands should grasp the thighs or remain in an upward position. To regain the feet, bounce from the back while extending the legs outward and downward. To perform the back drop from a bounce, lift the legs and hips upward simultaneously and as the performer begins the drop to the canvas, he should follow the same procedure as described above.

Half-Twist to Front Drop

Bounce upward lifting the hips and legs as if going into a back-drop. Perform a half-turn by dropping the shoulder and looking in the direction that you wish to turn. As the turn is made, pike at the hips and hold the pike until the drop is almost completed. Just prior to contact with the canvas, extend the body for the front-drop position.

Half-Twist to Back Drop

Bounce upward and lean forward as if going into a front drop. Lower one shoulder and raise the other while looking in the direction of the lower one. As the twist is completed, maintain a pike position with the eyes looking toward the knees and perform the back drop.

Combination-Front Drop to Back Drop

Perform the front drop and push hard with the hands and forearms, thus driving the head and chest upward and backward. As the head and chest rise, bend at the knees and waist and continue to lean backwards until the back position is achieved.

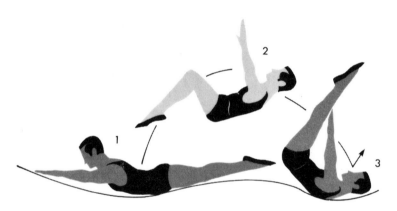

Combination-Back Drop to Front Drop

Perform the back drop and kick upward and outward with the legs. As the head and shoulders rise and the feet drop downward, maintain a pike at the hips until just prior to contact with the mat. To contact the mat, stretch the body out of the pike position and land in the front-drop position.

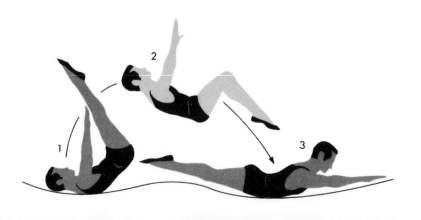

Seat Drop Half-Twist to Feet

Perform a seat drop and push with the hands. As the performer bounces upward, he should lift the hands overhead and drive the feet and legs downward. As the performer reaches the peak of his bounce, he should perform a half-twist by turning the head and shoulders in the direction he wishes to turn. At the completion of the turn, the performer lands on the feet.

Seat Drop Half-Twist to Seat

This stunt is performed in the same manner as the preceding stunt, except as the performer completes the half-twist, he bends at the hips and performs another seat drop.

Back Drop Half-Twist to Feet

Perform a back drop and as the legs are kicked upward and forward, turn the head and arms to the left or right, completing a half-turn. At the completion of the turn, land on the feet.

Back Drop Half-Twist to Seat Drop

This stunt is executed in the same manner as the preceding stunt, except that at the completion of the half-turn, the performer flexes the hips and lands in a seat-drop position.

Back Drop Half-Twist to Back Drop

Same as for the twist to feet, except that at the completion of the half-turn, the performer flexes the hips and leans backward landing in another back drop.

One-Half Turntable

Land in a front-drop position and push with the hands and knees while turning the head and shoulders to the left or right. While the turn is being made, the feet and head should be low with the hips high. As the turn is completed, the performer stretches out of the pike or tuck position for the landing in the front drop.

Front Somersault

From a bounce in the center of the mat, raise the arms and maintain them in an overhead position. As the feet again contact the mat, bounce upward, pushing the hips slightly backward and swinging the arms and head downward. The chin should be tucked to the chest and the body should be tucked at the knees and waist with the hands grasping the shins. As the body rotates and nears the upright position, the head should be raised and the body opened to a landing in the center of the mat. Avoid leaning too far forward as this will cause you to land several feet from where you started. The performer should first learn to somersault to the back and seat successfully before attempting to land on the feet.

Back Pull-Over

Bounce upward, grasping the shins in a tight tuck position. As the performer drops to the mat, the seat and feet should contact the mat simultaneously. On the upward bounce, the performer pulls on the shins and rolls backwards, keeping the chin tucked close to the chest. As the body nears an upright position, the performer opens up and lands on the feet.

Routine

Combine as many of the above stunts as possible into a routine.

PHYSICAL PRINCIPLES INVOLVED IN REBOUND TUMBLING

A few of the scientific principles involved in executing stunts on the trampoline are listed as follows:

1. All essential turning movements start as the body leaves its point of support.

> **Example:** To execute a forward somersault, there must be some lean forward to get the center of gravity ahead of the feet on takeoff in order to produce the necessary rotation.

2. The speed of turning is controlled by the length of the radius of rotation about the center of gravity.

> **Example:** In turning a somersault, the shorter the radius (tighter the tuck) the faster the rotating velocity.

3. For every force there is always an equal and opposite counterforce.

> **Example:** As the performer leaves the bed of the trampoline, his legs must be extended and his body rigid so as to produce the maximum reaction upward.

4. In performing basic-drop stunts, the center of gravity must be directed vertically so that it will be over the point from which the feet left the bed when the body returns to the mat.

> **Example:** This principle is basic to such stunts as the seat, knee, back, and front drops.

5. The height to which the performer rises above the trampoline depends upon the amount the bed is depressed and the angle of takeoff.

> **Example:** This is evident when observing the difference in height between a straight vertical jump and a front somersault. Since some lean is needed for the somersault, the performer cannot attain maximum height.

6. The static balance of a body is indirectly proportional to the distance of the center of gravity of that body above its base.

> **Example:** In making a steady stop from a high bounce on the trampoline, bend at the knees and waist as you contact the bed. This lowers the center of gravity and kills the spring by spending the force of the landing over a distance.

7. Equilibrium is directly proportional to the area of the base on which the body is supported.

> **Example:** In bouncing on the trampoline, the feet should land on the bed a pace apart, as opposed to together, so that greater stability can be obtained.

INDEX